MW00826142

KERBSTONE MERCHANTS

Some people make collections
Of fossils, eggs and ferns
Of coins, and stamps, and butterflies
And other things by turns.

But Uncle's more original
Than anyone you'll meet,
For he collects the penny toys
They sell you in the street.

Wherever crowds are thickest
These merchants stand all day,
With every kind of 'novelty'
Spread out upon a tray.

And Uncle takes his business bag
And buys from every one,
Though he once bought a running mouse
And couldn't make it run.

E V Lucas, c.1905

THE BOOK OF

PENNY TOYS

DAVID PRESSLAND

with additional material by Ian Leonard

NEW CAVENDISH BOOKS
LONDON

Dedicated to the memory of the late Barney Barenholtz

First edition published in Great Britain by New Cavendish Books

Designed by Jacky Wedgwood
Photography by Mark Williams

Editor Narisa Chakra
Production Allen Levy

Typeset by Dorchester Typesetting Group Limited, Dorset

Printed and bound in Hong Kong under the supervision of Mandarin Offset, London

ISBN 0 904568 54 7

The title page illustration shows an Edwardian Christmas card depicting a boy selling penny toys.

Acknowledgements

The author's grateful thanks are due to the following:

Tim Armitage; Carlernst Baecker for permission to reproduce catalogue pages from the *Die Anderen Nurnberger* series; Dr Lydia Bayer, curator of the Nuremberg Toy Museum, Monica Burckhardt, Conservateur Musée des Arts Decoratifs, Paris, for help to both authors in their researches; Pierce Carlson; Chambre Syndicate des Fabricants de Jouets et Jeux, Paris, for access to their records; Stuart and Linda Cropper; John Haley; Hilary Kay, for continual encouragement and help reading text and correcting proofs; Clive Lamming; Allen Levy; Colin Manton, Museum of London, for help with study and photography of items from the King Collection; Jill Martin, for bringing her collection of celluloid penny toys to London for photography; Patrick Rylands, for loan of items from his collection for photography; Hasso Wien.

Also to Sally Melvin for her inspired backdrops to the chapter opening photographs in the Tinplate section; to Mark Williams, for his superb photography, his enthusiasm and care in handling the toys; to Jacky Wedgwood for her design which helps to show the toys to their best advantage; finally, to Narisa Chakra for her editorial guidance and unique offer of typing the author's manuscript. This offer was gratefully accepted although well beyond the call of editorial duty.

CONTENTS

TINPLATE

OTHER MATERIALS

IDENTIFICATION

INTRODUCTION

"THEY ARE like the cries of London. They belong only to yesterday but two World Wars have made the actuality of the penny toy recede into what seems to be antiquity. Penny Toys! There's a rhythmic magic in the very phrase that would never sound as hypnotic if we said 'ha'penny' or 'tupenny'. Penny rattle! Penny whistle! This is the very coinage of late Victorian or Edwardian childhood, surviving only in its storybooks and jingles."

This was the late Leslie Daiken's eloquent introduction to an article he wrote in the Christmas issue of *The Illustrated London News* published in November 1957. Entitled "Only one penny – and all one penny: Penny Toys – the delight of children in the past and a lasting record of changing fashions", it was illustrated with items from the Ernest King collection then housed in Kensington Palace but now in the Museum of London. It is a fascinating article untainted by any of the pretentiousness that collector's values bring and is based on a nostalgia for penny toys and their role as a reflection of social history.

When the author wrote *The Art of the Tin Toy* in 1976, penny toys were defined as "small toys sold at a retail price of one penny principally in the years between 1895 and 1914." In the light of research done during the writing of this book, they should now be defined as "small toys designed to be sold at a retail price of one penny principally in the years between 1890 and 1935."

Apart from the extension of the dates the important change in the definition is the insertion of the words 'designed to be'. This has proved necessary as in the King collection there are several toys that undoubtedly cost more than a penny originally which must have been old warehouse stock that had been acquired cheaply by the penny toy street vendors from whom he acquired all his collection. The other difficulty with the definition has been accounting for the effects of inflation. The range and quality of toys that could be purchased in 1900 for a penny was much greater than in the 1920s and 1930s. Thus some toys sold for a penny early in the century could no longer be classified as penny toys in the 1920s.

Ernest King's collection is one man's record of purchasing penny objects in London. His collecting rule was simple – to buy one of anything that was available for a penny. The King collection's importance lies not so much in the objects it contains but in the two notebooks that King kept, logging the dates of each purchase. These notebooks are entitled *City Street Peno'rths* – a marvellously Dickensian title!

The first object was bought on 16 February 1893 and the last (No 1703), a red white and blue favour for Armistice Day on 11 November 1918. Although known as a collection of penny toys, a substantial part of the 1703 objects are not toys at all, but badges, combs, souvenirs, etc. In amongst the many ephemeral objects there is a fine collection of penny toys. The notebooks provide us with much interesting information. Statistically it is interesting to note that in terms of objects bought per year, the peak period was in the middle of the first decade of the twentieth century. The following are examples of the number of objects bought in each year.

1893	32
1894	92
1900	23
1904	219
1906	168
1908	104
1916	23

It is also interesting to note that November and December were the peak buying months. For example, out of 168 objects bought in 1906, 86 were bought in December. Obviously not too much must be read into these statistics, as they do not state how active Ernest King was in his purchasing at any given time. However, certain trends do emerge. Many of the well known tin penny toys were purchased in 1904 and 1905 suggesting that this is when they first appeared for sale. The figures also suggest that the period 1904 to 1908 was the peak time for the introduction of new toys and other objects and also that November and December were the key months for new stock to appear. This latter statistic might appear obvious in view of Christmas, but it is interesting to see it confirmed.

King bought all his collection from the street vendors in London for whom he obviously had great sympathy. There are several press cuttings contained in his notebooks outlining the plight of the street vendors when they were evicted from Ludgate Hill in December 1908. The Lowther Arcade (off the Strand) was another area where penny toys could be bought. Certainly in London, street vendors were one of the principal sources for penny toys. They were also sold in regular toy stores as toys, Christmas tree decorations, sweet containers or dispensers, or in boxes as party giveaways.

Penny toys were production line items. Most diecast toys came from Simon and Rivollet or other smaller factories in Paris; most tinplate toys from factories in and around Nuremberg; most wooden toys from the traditional wood carving areas of Germany – Erzgebirge and Sonneberg. Many of the mixed media toys came from Japan. The paper games and celluloid toys generally came from Germany. Many penny toys were made from natural materials – 'London in a nutshell' is a dried walnut shell containing a fold-out sheet of souvenir photographs.

Distribution was invariably via wholesalers to export markets all over the world. The use of tin penny toys as either sweet containers or as a promotional sales aid, particularly at Easter and Christmas, was a very important method of distribution and sale. The larger department stores sold mixed penny toys in boxes of 48 or 100 to be used as Christmas tree decorations or as party giveaways. The simpler penny toys and the more elaborate cracker toys overlap and become impossible to differentiate.

As already mentioned, penny toys can be made of many different materials and the following is a chart of the approximate percentages of the various materials used in objects found in the King collection:

Material	%
Paper	17.6 %
Diecast	9.1 %
Wire/badges etc	11.0 %
Wood	5.5 %
Tinplate (toy)	13.3 %
Tinplate (non toy)	8.3 %
Other materials	35.2 %

Included in other materials are cotton, china, leather, matches, beads, chalk, nuts, shells, silk, wool, glass, plaster, celluloid and many other substances.

This chart clearly demonstrates that diecast and tinplate penny toys which are the most important for today's collectors formed together less than 25% of the penny objects sold. Many of the very ephemeral objects made of paper, feathers, bamboo, plaster and silk are catalogued as being Japanese in origin. None of the tin penny toys were readily identifiable as being Japanese. The huge majority of the King tin penny toys are German with just a few French examples included. On the other hand most of the diecast penny toys were French in origin.

Aside from Ernest King, there was considerable interest in penny toys at the turn of the century. This is reflected in the publication of such books as Gordon Craig's *Book of Penny Toys* and Mabel Dearmer's *The Book of Penny Toys* (1), both published in 1899.

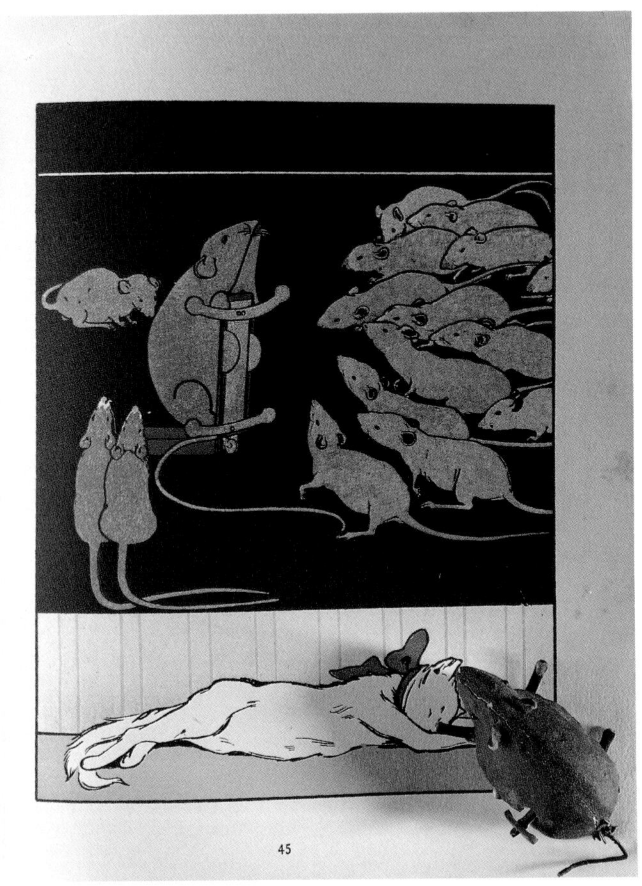

1 Page from Mabel Dearmer's *Book of Penny Toys* and clockwork mouse

This interest stems more from their sociological significance than their importance as collectable items. Just as early nineteenth century mechanization had brought manufactured goods for the newly formed middle class to buy, so the mass production of cheap but attractive and amusing penny toys brought toys within the means of all but the poorest families. Thus their importance lay not so much in themselves, as in the fact that they represented one of the first non-essential luxuries for the poorer members of society.

It comes as a surprise to find that despite the huge interest in all collectable objects today, no book on penny toys has been written in the past fifty years. For many years collectors have looked forward to a book being published on the subject. Despite having a large penny toy collection myself, I have been reluctant to tackle the subject as the more I have learned about penny toys, the more I realize how little I know. However, by recording the knowledge I have acquired over many years collecting, I hope that this book will act as a foundation on which others can build.

There was an immense variety in the different penny toys produced and I would estimate that there are at least as many again as those that have been pictured. It would be virtually impossible to catalogue and illustrate every penny toy and its variations and one would run the risk of becoming somewhat repetitive.

Ian Leonard and I were talking about our respective collections during a quiet moment at one of the Beaulieu Autojumbles, when Ian volunteered to write and illustrate from his own collection the sections on diecast, wood, paper and celluloid penny toys, if I would write the section on tinplate penny toys. I thought back to a conversation I had had with the late Barney Barenholtz (one of America's legendary toy collectors), standing in front of a showcase of penny toys the last time he visited my home. Barney, being the perfect gentleman, said "You would do us all a great favour if you would write a book on penny toys." The fire was kindled and, after a feasibility study over lunch with Narisa Chakra and Allen Levy, work began.

David Pressland 1990

EXPLANATORY NOTES

1 TINPLATE

Rarity

Each photograph of a tinplate penny toy is numbered, this number being shown in bold type. After the number is a capital letter denoting the relative rarity of the toy. The question of rarity is inevitably a very debatable subject that can only reflect the author's opinion at this time:

A Very rare and few known
B Rare and difficult to find
C Obtainable but not always easily
D Readily obtainable
E Common

Most penny toys will fall into the middle categories. Few fall into the A category as all were mass-produced, although some had a short life span. Few also can be classified in the E category as all were fragile and generally not treated with much respect by their youthful first owner. Thus a very small percentage of the millions produced originally have survived. It is certain that the gradings will need to be amended over the years to come. The author remembers many years ago that the Kellermann pool player (**476**) was considered quite rare until a box of 144 was found in the United States and a glut of mint examples appeared on the market!

These gradings do not necessarily reflect desirability, which is obviously a personal judgement. Generally, early brightly lithographed toys are more desirable than later dull examples. A very rare but rather plain penny toy might be much less desirable than a relatively common, but very attractive penny toy such as Meier's gnome and parrot (**381**). Value is always a combination of rarity, condition, desirability and demand, and it is always best left for the market place to be the final arbiter.

Many tin penny toys both common and rare have had to be omitted from this book through lack of space. It must not be assumed that any penny toy not included is automatically rare.

Dimensions

After the rarity coding, is a dimension which is given in millimetres (25.4 mm = 1 inch). This dimension refers to the overall length, unless the height is greater than the length, in which case 'high' is specified.

Attribution

The maker's name is given in the caption relating to the toy. Where this is unequivocably stated there is reasonable proof that this is correct. Where a question mark or the words 'possibly' or 'probably' appear there is no proof, but it is the author's considered opinion from a careful study of catalogues and the toy itself that the maker is as attributed. Where no maker can be attributed at this time, the country of origin is given when possible.

Condition

Condition is of extreme importance. Lithographed penny toys cannot be properly restored. A rusted, faded or scratched lithographed penny toy, however rare, is not very attractive or desirable. This is an unfortunate fact of collecting life. As with all clouds, the silver lining is the fact that it is uneconomic to reproduce lithographed penny toys. Certain parts such as wheels can be readily changed and parts from two penny toys can be married together to make a very effective and unique toy (**486**), but the chances of being caught out by a complete forgery are very remote indeed.

2 OTHER MATERIALS

Bibliographic references

As in Part 1, picture numbers are shown in bold type. Bracketed numbers not in bold type indicate bibliographic references which can be found in the numbered bibliography.

Measurements

Measurements given refer to the largest dimension of the object. Where several objects are grouped together the measurements are expressed as a range from the smallest to the largest object.

Note: There is no plate **422**.

TINPLATE

THE DIFFICULTY of defining a penny toy has already been discussed in the general introduction. Two further difficulties arise specifically with tinplate toys. These can be summarized as follows:

1 **Quality variations** The same toy could be produced in more than one quality (i.e. an automobile with or without mudguards, with or without extra figures, with or without a flywheel). Such distinctions are generally all considered to be variants. The addition of a clockwork motor to a toy car, however, technically makes it no longer a penny toy as its initial selling price would have been double. Nevertheless, many collectors still include such toys in their collections.

2 **Size variations** Many well known penny toy cars and boats particularly those by Distler and Fischer were also produced in a slightly larger size which probably sold for two pennies. These larger size toys, although identical in shape, style and method of construction, are not true penny toys and cannot be classified as such.

True tinplate penny toys, generally spirit-painted, first appeared for sale in the latter part of the nineteenth century. They may have been produced in small factories or assembled at home by families of outworkers. Certainly the standard and accuracy of painting was poor. The advent of offset lithography was the single most important development in the history of the tin penny toy, as it enabled superb detail and colour to be applied to a tinplate surface quickly and economically. Before this, the two main printing methods were:

a Direct printing from the lithographic stone or typemetal on to the tinplate. The principal drawback to this method was that with two non-absorbent surfaces, the ink did not take properly.

b Transfer printing whereby the design was printed on to thin transfer paper and thence onto the tinplate.

Offset lithography was patented in 1875 by Robert Barclay and John Doyle Fry, partners in the printing house of Barclay & Fry in the City of London. (Henry Baker was working on a similar process at the same time in Paris.) The original offset lithography involved the printing of a design on a glazed cardboard blanket from which it was immediately offset onto the tinplate sheets. A further development was necessary before the process became commercially practicable, viz the substitution of a rubber-covered canvas sheet, and later a rubber composition roller, for the original glazed cardboard blanket. Barclay & Fry in turn licensed the use of their process to Huntley, Boorne and Stevens in Reading, but by 1889 the patent had lapsed, and from this date onwards the use of the process became almost universal.

The tinplate would be printed as flat sheets and then passed through a process that cut and formed the tinplate into self-coloured component parts ready for assembly by a relatively unskilled workforce. At times, tin penny toys are found where the cutting does not exactly follow the outline of the lithographic printing. This can seriously devalue a penny toy. This fault is rarely found on Meier's toys of the pre-1914 era.

The initiating costs of preparing lithographic plates and press tools was high but when spread over a production run that might run into the hundreds of thousands, the unit cost could be kept low. A highly skilled team of artists and tool makers would be required to initiate production.

Parisian and German spirit-painted penny toys from the 1890s were probably produced in roughly similar numbers.

The French toys were generally produced in many different small factories and these were slow to introduce offset lithography. The German penny toy makers were fewer and larger and introduced lithography around the turn of the century. At first, just parts of spirit-painted toys were lithographed (i.e. a driver on a car or a horse pulling a cab), but within a few years lithography was universally applied. This enabled the German factories to produce very detailed and beautiful toys very economically and by the middle of the first decade of the twentieth century they were dominant, exporting, via wholesalers, vast quantities of penny toys all over the world.

During the 1920s and 1930s many tin penny toys were produced in Japan by several different makers. Some of these were near clones of German penny toys. Others were totally oriental in design and execution. These Japanese penny toys were generally exported to markets geographically close to Japan and to the United States. Rather fewer were exported to Europe. Paya, in Spain, was a prolific penny toy maker producing many near copies of German penny toys. The quality of lithography on these Spanish penny toys is of a high standard and they make an interesting comparison with their German counterparts. Paya did not export widely. In Italy, copies of Meier penny toys were also made.

Tinplate German penny toys are by far the most numerous both in overall numbers and in terms of different designs produced. They were succinct mirror images of a rapidly changing world. Many had very short production runs and consequently are rare today. Others were produced for as long as 25–30 years, although the earlier examples are of better quality.

The most attractive penny toys are those dating from about 1900 to 1912. At this period the tinplate used was thickly plated and had an almost mirror-like finish. This can be clearly seen on the plain underside of early toys. When this high quality tinplate was used in combination with a new crisp lithographic plate, the finish attained was superb. This finish had a silvery gold transluscence which enhances the sharp lithographic detail. The identical toy produced in the mid-1920s has a dull finish as it was printed on a much lower grade tinplate and the lithographic plate may well have been old and worn, thus producing a dull, slightly smudged effect. The desirability of the earlier toy is much greater.

Tin penny toys were generally sold and distributed by wholesalers, but they were also sold to other toy manufacturers for use as component parts of larger toys such as carousels or steam accessories. Meier was almost exclusively a penny toy manufacturer and made only a few larger size toys. However, Meier made boxed sets including the military set illustrated in plate 2 and several boxed train sets containing one, two or three carriages. The best known boxed penny toy sets are those produced by J W Spear and Sohne of Nuremberg. These include 'Toy Town

2 A boxed military set by Meier

Airship Meet', 'Toy Town Garage' (3) and 'Toy Town Railroad' (4). The latter set was available in a smaller size as well. These sets contained penny toys by Meier, Hess and Distler. In the USA, they were marketed and distributed by Parker Brothers and the J W Spear origin of the toys was not mentioned. Other manufacturers produced sets, incorporating penny toys including fire engines with cast firemen and military vehicles with cast soldiers.

To aid the location of penny toys in this section, the book has been divided into chapters that either reflect the subject matter (eg Automotive) or the function (eg Whistles) of the individual toys. In many cases it was immediately clear into which chapter to place a certain toy. In other cases there were as many as three chapters into which a toy could have been placed. In this case I have tried to place the toy in the chapter that best reflects its primary subject matter or function. For example plate **342** is a toy which is a rabbit containing a whistle, while at the same time being a candy container. This toy could have been included in the 'Animal', 'Whistles', or 'Bank, Building and Candy Containers' chapters. It was decided that this toy's main design and function was as a candy container and accordingly the reader will find it there. Many other toys, particularly in the Automotive and Fantasy chapters, contain compartments that could be used to hold candy, but in these instances, this feature was considered to be secondary.

3 'Toy Town Garage' by Spear & Sohne

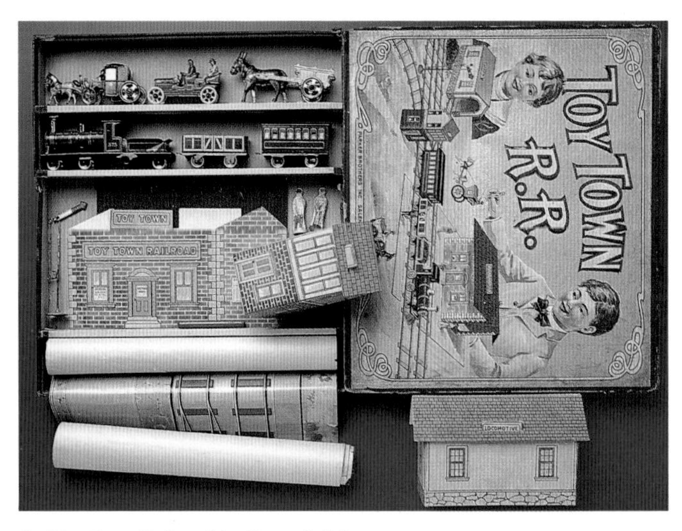

4 'Toy Town Railroad' by Spear & Sohne

ANIMAL

5 B 72 mm

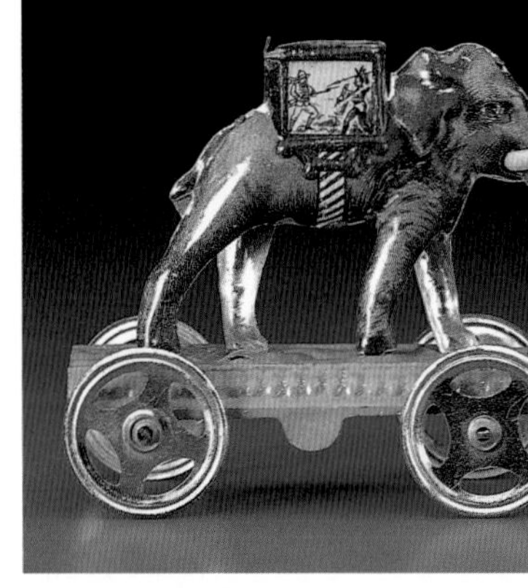

6 C 75 mm

All the animals shown here were made by Meier. The gold coloured elephant which was made in the late nineteenth century forms an interesting comparison with **6** which dates from a few years later. Note the unstable wheels and spirit-painting on the earlier toy and the improved lead centred wheels and lithographic detail on the later toy. In all three animals with packs, a sliding removeable lid permitted their use as a candy container. The goat has a mechanical rocking action as it is pushed along.

7 C 75 mm

8 C 75 mm

Detail of **6**

Four animals by Meier. The flat non-wheeled naturalistic green base was used with many of the other animals from the Meier range. It is less commonly found than the wheeled bases and circumstantial evidence points to the fact that it was only produced for a few years prior to 1914. Meier animals are also commonly found with the flat base and small red wheels. This dates from both before and after the First World War being in fact used to the end of Meier's production in the mid-1930s.

9 C 70 mm

10 C 70 mm

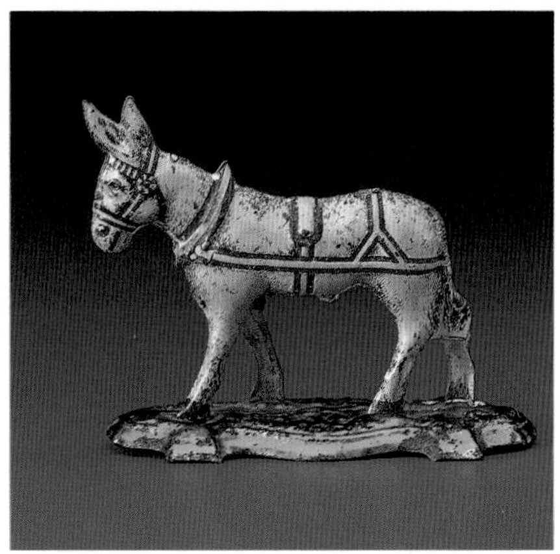

11 C 70 mm

12 D 80 mm

Eight Meier animals featuring the plain red-wheeled base. All are non-mechanical and most were made pre-1914 and again in the 1920s. Several of these penny toys are shown in the 1924 *Universal Toy Catalogue* on page 18. The deer with the weighted, articulating head may not have been made post-1918.

13 C 90 mm

14 C 85 mm

15 C 80 mm

16 D 80 mm

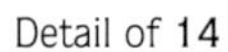

Detail of **14**

17 B 78 mm

18 C 85 mm

19 C 80 mm

20 C 83 mm

Detail of **17**

21 B 75 mm

22 C 75 mm

Four Meier penny toys which all had long production runs and were available on more than one type of base.

23 C 75 mm

24 C 72 mm

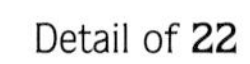

Detail of **22**

Geese and swans were a popular subject for the German penny toy makers. Several of these makers featured toys of geese with articulated weighted heads and these are some of the commonest penny toys found. **26** is by Meier, **25** is by Distler and **27** and **28** are by unidentified manufacturers.

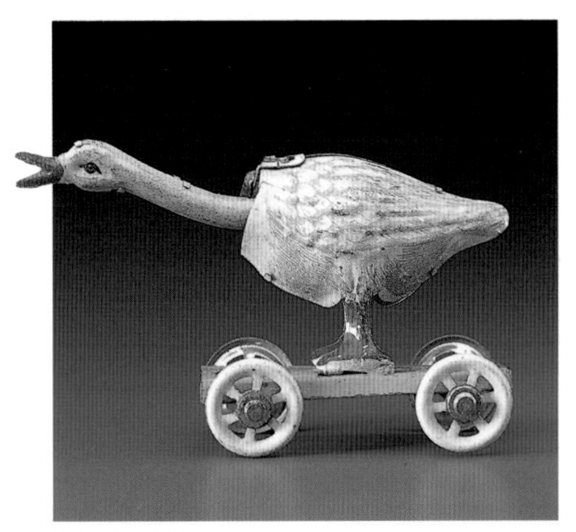

25 D 100 mm

26 C 75 mm

27 C 103 mm

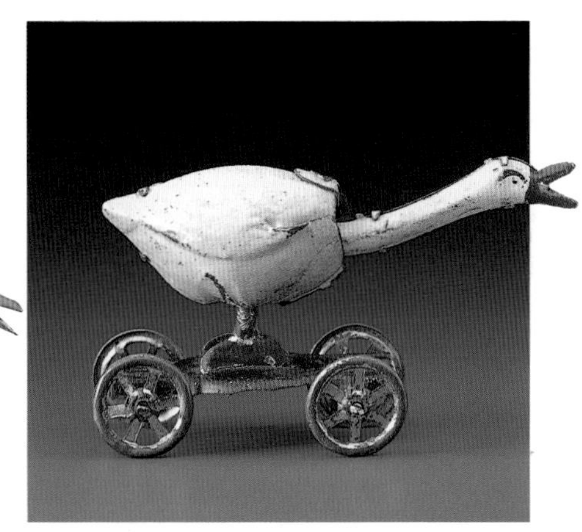

28 C 93 mm

Detail of **26**

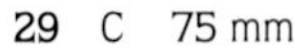

29 C 75 mm

30 B 75 mm

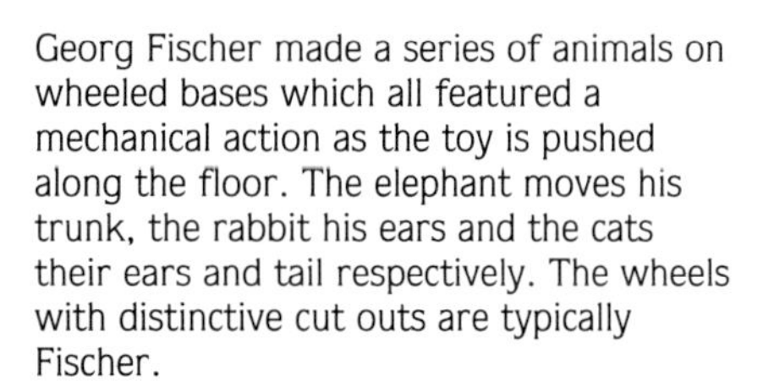

Georg Fischer made a series of animals on wheeled bases which all featured a mechanical action as the toy is pushed along the floor. The elephant moves his trunk, the rabbit his ears and the cats their ears and tail respectively. The wheels with distinctive cut outs are typically Fischer.

31 C 75 mm

32 C 75 mm

Detail of **30**

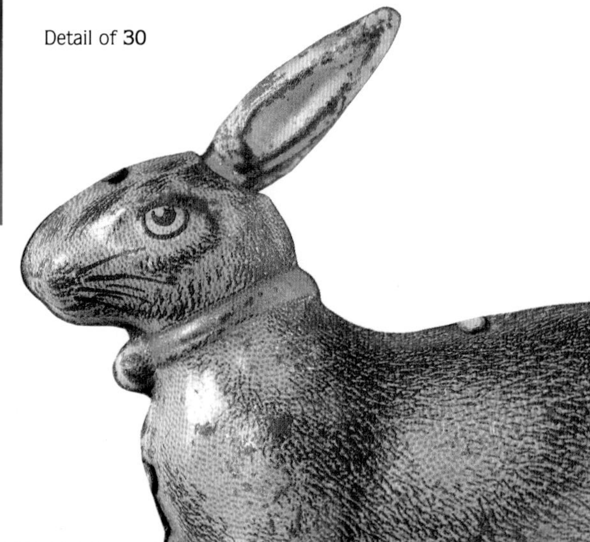

33 This has Fischer type wheels but cannot be definitely attributed to that company.

34 Features a nodding head. It has several Meier characteristics but cannot be conclusively attributed to this manufacturer.

35, 36 Two toys in the Georg Fischer series of mechanical animals. The donkey's ears move and the bird rocks back and forth to imitate a pecking action.

33 D 80 mm

34 C 80 mm

35 C 75 mm

36 C 75 mm

Detail of **36**

37 C 85 mm

38 C 80 mm

39 C 83 mm

40 C 70 mm

Distler produced a whole range of animals with spring tails or in the case of the elephant a spring trunk. The cow has a conventional tin tail but is also by Distler. All these penny toys were made both before 1914 and again in the 1920s.

41 C 62 mm

42 C 65 mm

43 B 72 mm

44 C 75 mm

Detail of **39**

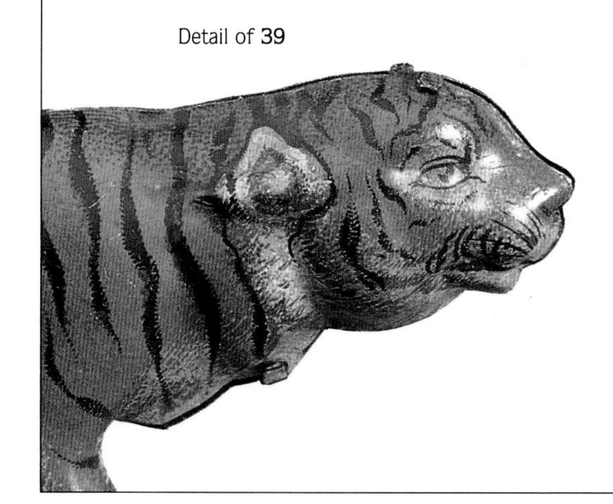

45 B 57 mm

46 B 68 mm

47 C 60 mm

48 B 75 mm

49 B 75 mm

45–47 These three toys feature high quality lithography and can be attributed to the manufacturer who used the initials HMN as a trademark. The harlequin Great Dane should be carrying a bucket in his mouth. None of the toys are marked but the Great Dane features on page 345 of *The Universal Toy Catalogue*. The other two toys have parts in common with the Great Dane.

48, 49 Two attractive pre-1914 penny toys which are stamped on the base sides with the initials IJF. This manufacturer who also produced the red racing car featured in plate **149** has not as yet been identified.

50 C 110 mm

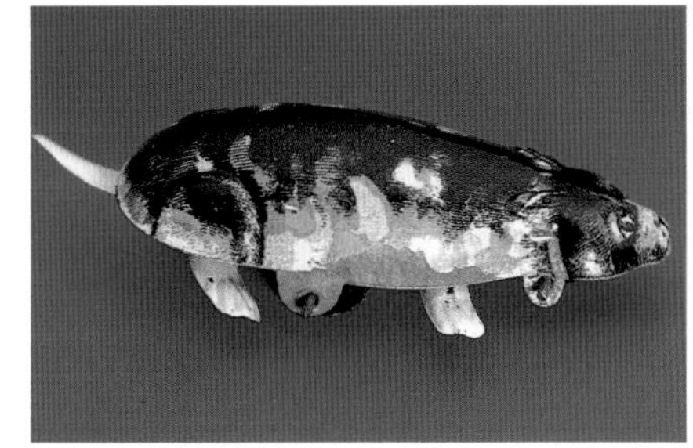

51 C 85 mm

52 D 85 mm

Gebr Einfalt did not start in business until 1922 but their range of simple penny toys appear to have been very successful in the 1920s and 1930s. Einfalt supplied several items to UTCC in Chicago. The quality of pressings and lithography was poor compared to pre-1914 penny toys.

The mouse and cat both feature in the page of Einfalt toys (page 26) in the 1924 *Universal Toy Catalogue*. The pigeon has Einfalt characteristics but cannot be definitely attributed to the company.

In plate **53** the larger beetles, butterfly, tortoise and lizard can be definitely attributed to Einfalt. The smaller beetles have a higher standard of finish and may also be by Einfalt but this is by no means certain.

53 D–E 40–120 mm

54 C 125 mm wingspan

55 C 120 mm wingspan

56 D 65 mm

Three examples of French penny toys. The monkey riding on the poodle is made of wool and wire (not dissimilar to a pipe cleaner) attached to a conventional tin base. There are many different penny toys of this type. There is an indecipherable embossed logo on the base which might be CR. The golden fly (la mouche d'or) has a cast body and sprung tin wings. Again the base plate has an indecipherable logo. **54** is a mechanical moth which flaps its wings as it is pushed along.

HORSEDRAWN

57 A 115 mm

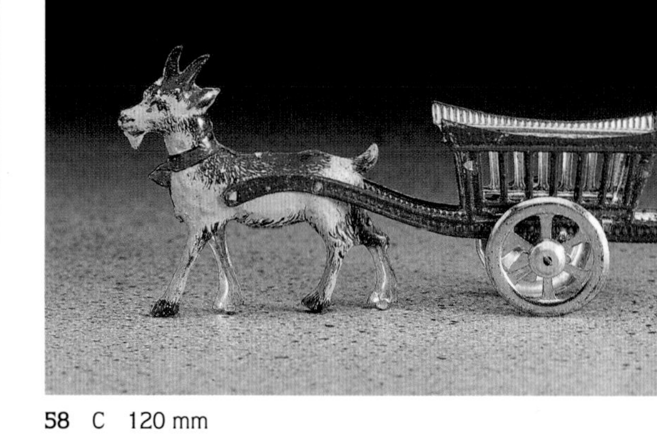

58 C 120 mm

59 B 120 mm

60 B 125 mm

All four toys were made by Meier. The spirit-painted horse and cart depicted in plate **57** is particularly early and dates from the 1890s. The dog cart is an interesting choice of toy as it is an exact copy of Meier's trademark. It would be very exciting to find out the reasons behind Meier's choice of trademark. The sleigh (**60**) could be used as a candy container.

61 C 150 mm

62 C 80 mm

63 C 175 mm

64 B 110 mm

61, 62 This Meier cart is found in many different forms and at least two different sizes. It was available both with and without animals. Originally made in the 1890s, it undoubtedly had a long production run.

63 Another cart by Meier which is more commonly found drawn by a horse (see **65**).

64 An unusual German penny toy featuring a well lithographed but rather flat goat and a very plain sleigh on wheels. The manufacturer has not been identified.

65 C 140 mm

66 B 115 mm

67 B 145 mm

68 B 120 mm

Seven of these penny toys were made by Meier; the eighth (**71**) has many Meier characteristics, but no one feature that permits a definite attribution. Many of these toys are made of embossed metal which was commonly used by Meier to show details prior to the widespread use of lithography. This can be clearly seen on the

69 C 155 mm

70 C 155 mm

71 C 150 mm

72 C 140 mm

three fire toys and the postal van. The two Grand Hotel omnibuses are lithographed. They are not just colour variations – the people portrayed in the windows are also different. The Grand Hotel omnibus was also sold without a horse in both variants. The horseless version was made with two different forms of shaft.

73 C 120 mm

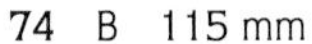

74 B 115 mm

Detail of **73**

Both these cabs were also available contemporaneously as motorized vehicles. The blue cab (**73**) is by Meier and features a stern-looking Victorian father at one window and his wife and child at the other. The red cab (**74**) is possibly by Fischer (see **125**). Both vehicles date from the 1902–1914 period.

Detail of **73**

75 D 110 mm

76 C 120 mm

75 A commonly found cab of rather poor quality whose manufacturer has not been identified.

76 This was also available as a motorized cab. Fischer may have been the manufacturer.

77 A very elegant cab with finely detailed horse and driver. Made by Fischer in the pre-1914 era.

77 B 120 mm

78 C 107 mm

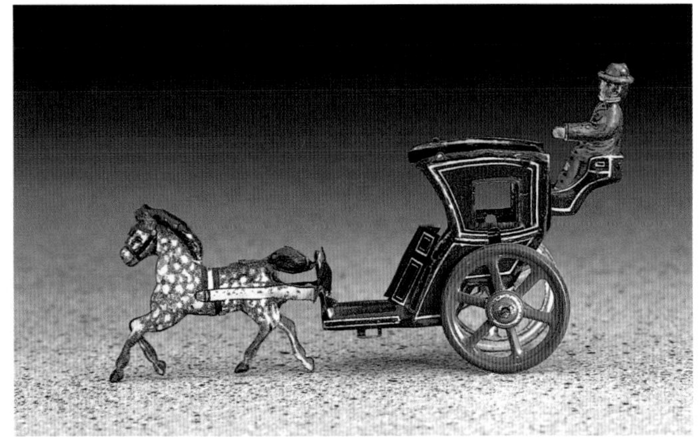

79 C 115 mm

80 C 130 mm

78 Meier's interpretation of a hansom cab.

79 A very attractive and stylish hansom cab which is not uncommon but whose maker is not yet known.

80 An interesting cab whose manufacturer is as yet unidentified. The bottom slides out to enable the cab to act as a sweet container.

Detail of 79

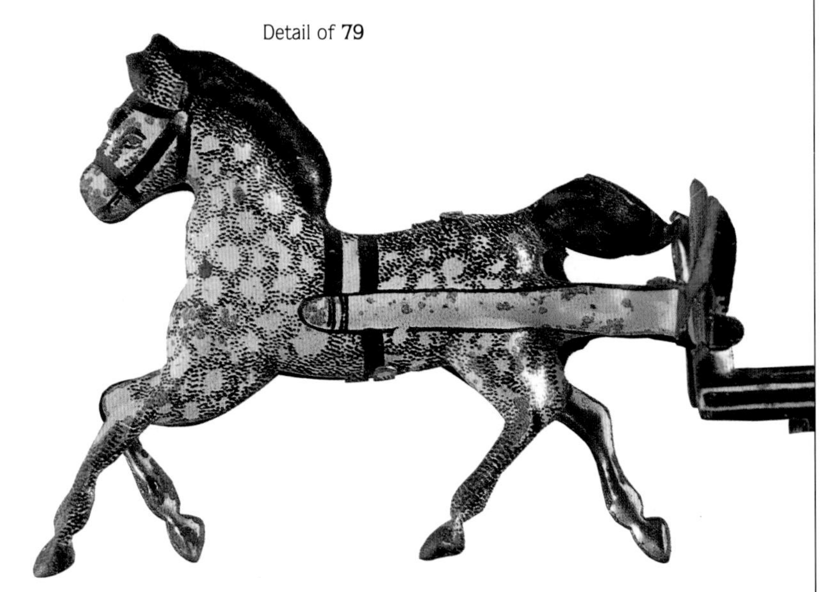

81 C 135 mm

82 C 126 mm

The landau (**81**) and carriage (**82**) are both by Meier. The raffia reins shown in plate **81** are probably original. The third carriage (**83**) is almost certainly by Fischer. All three of these toys were available both pre and post the 1914–18 war.

83 B 124 mm

84 D 120 mm

85 D 105 mm

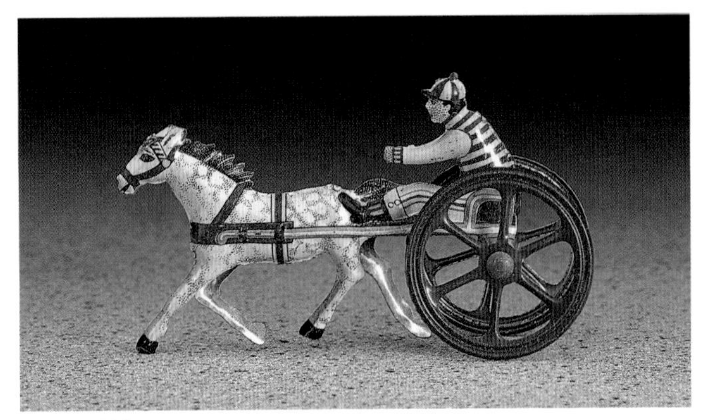

86 C 110 mm

87 C 90 mm

84, 85 Two simple French spirit-painted carriages whose manufacturer has not been identified.

86 A very stylish trotting car by Meier.

87 Another trotting car probably made by Distler, both before and after the First World War.

88 A 115 mm

89 C 110 mm

90 A 105 mm

It would be very interesting to know what the minimum order had to be to have a penny toy specially commissioned for advertising or publicity purposes. The Anthony Hordern & Sons of Sydney covered delivery wagon must have been a special order. I believe that the No. 14 Horse Ambulance provided by the 'Our Dumb Friends League' could have been a promotional toy for this English charity. Both these toys have Distler-like features, but neither can be definitely attributed to this manufacturer. The horses on the ambulance were taken from a Meier penny toy as the originals were missing when the toy was found.

89 A Meier horsedrawn cart that was also available in a motorized version. Note the chain drive has not been removed for the horsedrawn version!

91 C 160 mm

92 C 110 mm

93 D 120 mm

94 D 125 mm

91, 92 Both toys are by Meier.

93, 94 These are two of the commonest early penny toys found, yet neither can be definitely attributed to a manufacturer with certainty. Fischer may have been responsible for **94** as the wheels are typical.

95 C 95 mm

96 C 95 mm

97 A 75 mm

98 D 130 mm

95, 96 Two removal wagons by Meier for the German and English markets respectively. I have never seen this toy with horses attached, but it is possible that Meier made it this way.

97 A well-lithographed souvenir of the 1911 Coronation of King George V and Queen Mary, whose portraits are depicted at the windows. Made by Distler, presumably in that year only.

98 This penny toy of an elephant pulling a cart was made by Fischer.

99 D 147 mm

100 D 147 mm

101 D 125 mm

102 C 115 mm

A series of eight variations on horsedrawn First World War equipment including ambulances, guns and limber, post van, etc. All were made by Meier. Each was either made with a driver and two riderless horses or with a mounted soldier and riderless horse. Examples of each style are depicted here.

103 C 120 mm

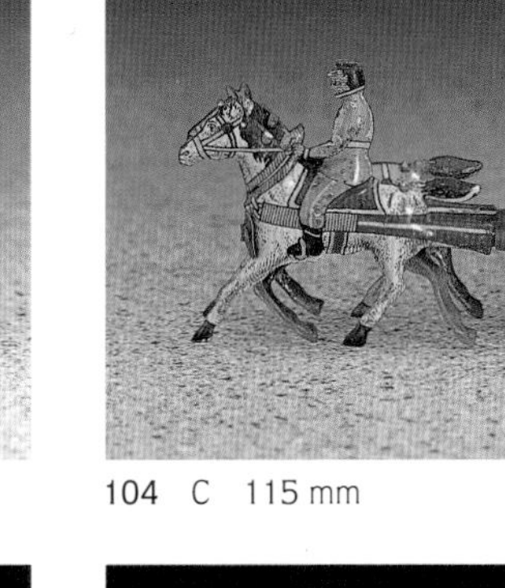

104 C 115 mm

105 C 115 mm

106 C 120 mm

107 B 105 mm

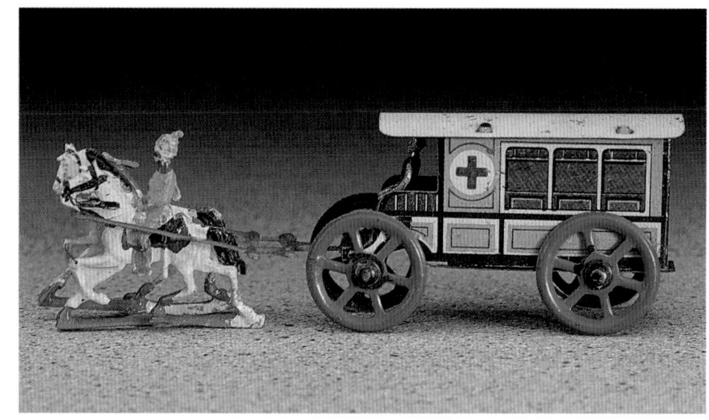

108 C 125 mm

109 C 120 mm

110 C 120 mm

107 An attractive ambulance probably by Fischer.

108–110 Three horsedrawn military toys which came in a boxed set with the trademark of Josef Bischoff of Nuremberg on the lid. Bischoff was a soldier maker and may well have bought the tin penny toys in from another manufacturer. The quality of the lithography on the ambulance is reminiscent of Hess (see Automotive plates **178, 179**).

AUTOMOTIVE

111 A 75 mm

112 D 75 mm

113 C 100 mm

114 B 115 mm

Detail of **114**

111 This early horseless carriage with dos-a-dos seating was almost certainly first produced by Meier in the late nineteenth century. It features tiller steering and a chauffeur more suitably dressed for a carriage and four. There is a compartment with sliding cover at the back, indicating that this penny toy could also be used as a candy container. The embossed painted side panels are typical of very early Meier toys.

112, 113 Two early twentieth century Meier cars. The smaller red vis-a-vis was produced up to the First World War and is one of the commonest of the 'veteran' period of penny toy car production.

114 A slightly larger scale clockwork car by an as yet unidentified manufacturer.

I am unable to attribute conclusively any of these cars to specific makers. The car pictured in **117** has high quality lithography reminiscent of Issmayer. Similarly the small car in plate **115** is certainly by the same maker as the locomotive depicted in plate **244** which I believe could also be Issmayer. The car in plate **118** is frequently found with either a clockwork mechanism or a flywheel. Some authorities have attributed it to Carette but equally the car could be by Issmayer.

115 B 80 mm

116 C 75 mm

117 B 110 mm

118 C 100 mm

119 D 85 mm

120 C 110 mm

121 C 85 mm

122 C 100 mm

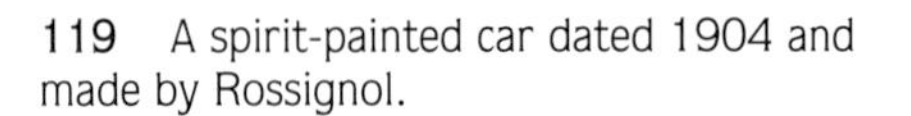

119 A spirit-painted car dated 1904 and made by Rossignol.

120 A real oddball! A six seater charabanc by Henri Avoiron of Paris.

121, 122 Both cars were probably made by Georg Fischer. A simplified version of **122** was made in the early 1920s.

123 I believe this to have been made by Georg Fischer. Its horsedrawn counterpart is depicted in plate **76**. The other three taxi cabs pictured are all motorized versions of horsedrawn cabs.

124 This one is by Meier and has identical body pressings to the horsedrawn version seen in plate **73**.

123 B 75 mm

124 C 81 mm

125 C 80 mm

126 C 85 mm

125 This taxicab has the initials FZ lithographed on the door. The wheels are typically Georg Fischer and I wonder if FZ could refer to Fischer, Zirndorf (a village close to Nuremberg). With all three of these vehicles it is certain that the horsedrawn cab and the motorized cab were available concurrently for many years.

126 Distler's taxicab was also available in white with gold lining.

127 B 95 mm

128 B 98 mm

129 C 105 mm

130 C 85 mm

127, 128 Fischer produced a series of very simple but extremely decorative cars which consisted of two matched pressings tabbed together. The figures were part of these two pressings. The only separate parts were the wheels and axles. These two cars must have been cheaper to produce than Meier's more complex two cars illustrated below. **127** was also available with a passenger who had a moveable right arm.

129, 130 The smaller Meier touring car is made up of ten separate pressings and the larger car of eight, excluding wheels and axles. Nevertheless, the Fischer racing car with its two simple pressings lacks nothing in style!

131 C 80 mm

132 C 95 mm

133 B 75 mm

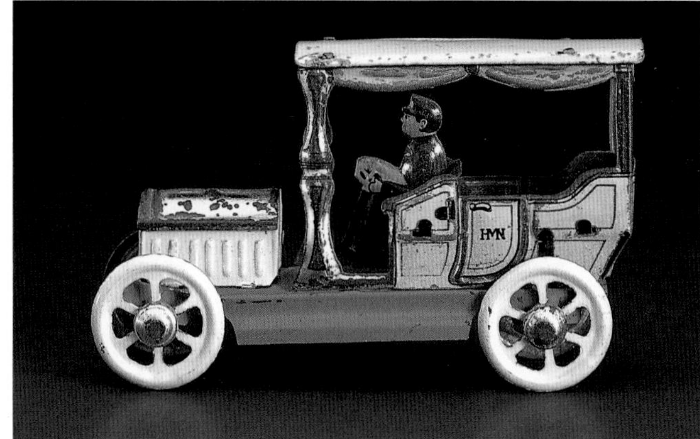

134 C 80 mm

131, 132 Two cars from Distler's pre-1914 production. Most of Distler's cars of this era were optionally available with a kangaroo as driver. The red open tourer featured an opening rear door.

133 A typical pre-1914 Fischer car which is very similar to its Distler counterpart.

134 An attractive high roof tonneau by HMN. Although of veteran styling, this toy was still available in 1925. It was also available without the roof.

135 B 70 mm

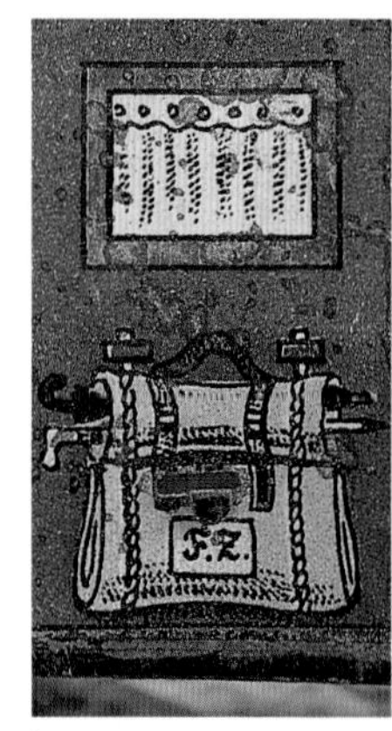

Detail of **135**

135, 136 These two high roof tonneaus have identical body pressings but a different lithographic finish. As with plate **125**, the trademark is FZ, which can be clearly seen in the detail photographs of the back lithography. The wheels on both these cars are typical Fischer.

137 A very small and simple toy car that was probably a cracker toy rather than a true penny toy. Note the wheels which are integral with the body pressings.

136 B 70 mm

Detail of **136**

137 D 40 mm

138 C 80 mm

139 C 80 mm

140 C 80 mm

141 B 75 mm

Four typical small limousines from the pre-1914 era. The two Meier cars (**138, 139**) are merely lithographic variants of the same car. It is surprising how frequently this occurs. They may have been produced concurrently, or one may be a replacement for the other when the printing plate had become worn. Certainly in this case, the finish of the white limousine is of a higher quality than the red one, leading to speculation that perhaps it is from the first plate, while the red is from the second less detailed one. The Distler limousine (**140**) has an opening door on the side shown. The fourth car (**141**) is by Georg Fischer.

142 C 110 mm

143 A 110 mm

144 B 100 mm

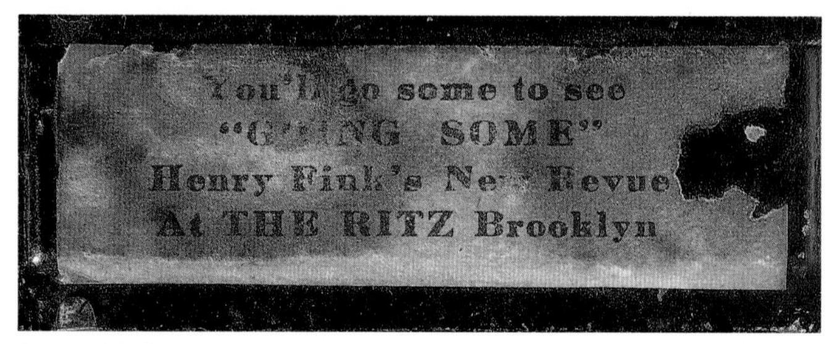

Detail of **143**

142, 143 Virtually identical limousines by Georg Fischer of Germany and CK of Japan. The Fischer car was available both with and without clockwork. The Japanese toy is undoubtedly a copy of the German one. Both date from the early 1920s. There is an interesting label stuck to the roof of the Japanese car advertising Henry Fink's new revue and it is possible that this toy was used as a promotional aid.

144 An attractive limousine by Issmayer dating from around 1912.

145 This Meier saloon features cut out passengers. This technique was in fashion for a short period and was also used by other manufacturers. A more finely detailed white and gold variation of this car also exists, but it does not have the vertical pin striping on the bodywork.

146, 147 Both cars are probably by Distler.

145 C 110 mm

146 C 110 mm

147 C 88 mm

148 C 95 mm

149 B 95 mm

150 C 110 mm

151 A 140 mm

Four stylish racing cars from the 'heroic' era of motor sport. **148** is a chain driven racer by Meier. **149** has the initials IJF printed on the radiator grill. I have not been able to identify this maker. The driver in this car comes from a Meier toy and is incorrect.

Both **150** and **151** are by Distler. The larger car features detailed instruments which are part of the main body pressing but have been bent round to face the driver.

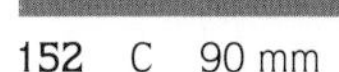

152 C 90 mm

153 C 90 mm

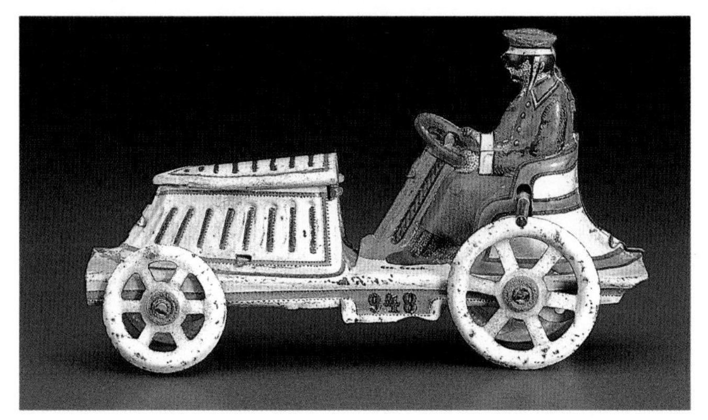

154 C 90 mm

155 B 90 mm

152, 153 These two cars were made by Georg Fischer and have similar body pressings. However in one the driver waves his arm and in the other he extends his neck as the car is pushed along.

154 This Meier car with simple pressings and driver incorporated into the bodywork is much more typical of Fischer. It may have represented Meier's attempt to cut production costs as competition from Fischer and Distler increased in the years leading up to the First World War.

155 Probably by Georg Fischer.

156 C 125 mm

157 D 100 mm

158 D 110 mm

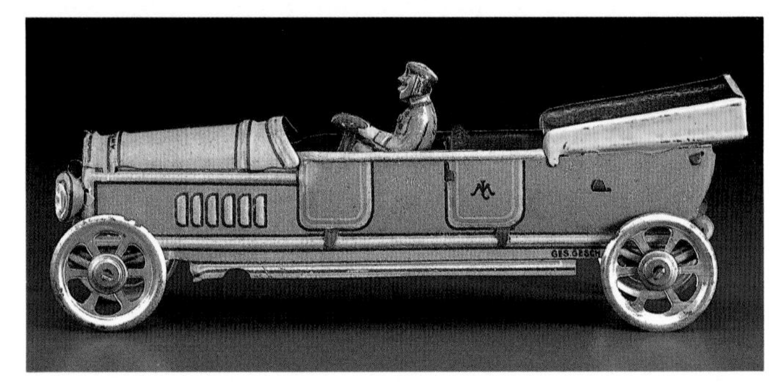

159 D 135 mm

156 A well-detailed penny toy representing an Edwardian touring car by Fischer.

157 This is also believed to be by Fischer.

158 Fischer's Mercedes based tourer dates from the 1920s.

159 This is a very simple and rather unattractive car made by Meier in the 1920s. The trademark has been incorporated into the lithography back to front. I am certain that such an error would never have slipped through in Johann Phillip Meier's lifetime. (Meier died in 1911 and, although many of the beautiful early penny toys continued to be made, it cannot be coincidental that there was a marked lack of imagination and quality in most of the new designs, particularly in the post 1914–1918 period.)

160 Fischer's early tricar is the only penny toy of this configuration I have seen. Like several early Fischer cars it consists of just two main pressings. The simplicity yet effectiveness of this design is remarkable.

161 A different type of tricar by an unknown maker. The box under the driver could be used as a sweet container.

162 This motorcycle combination is one of Distler's best penny toys. Certainly made in the 1920s it was probably produced prior to 1914 as well.

160 B 80 mm

161 B 90 mm

Detail of **162**

162 A 112 mm

163 C 70 mm

164 B 108 mm

165 B 108 mm

163–165 Three different Meier toys of Triumph motorcycles. The larger version was also available with just a solo rider.

166 C 100 mm

167 A 80 mm

166, 167 Two toys of the typically French 'triporteur'. 'Stop me and Buy One' was a familiar slogan to English children raised in the inter war years as it was used by virtually every ice cream vendor. This charming penny toy was made by Kellermann. The Express Triporteur (**166**) was made by Meier.

Detail of **166**

168 C 74 mm

168–170 Kellermann's penny toys were generally not the most visually exciting. However when it came to motorcycles Kellermann excelled. These three toys are all by this maker and were available in the 1920s. It is possible that one or all could have been made pre-1914 as well.

169 B 100 mm

170 B 103 mm

171 C 100 mm

172 C 100 mm

171, 172 Military and civilian versions of a motorcycle made by Meier.

173 This toy labelled IBENSE is of particular interest as it was made by Paya in Spain. Paya's catalogue of 1923 shows this and other penny toys many of which seem to be virtual copies of German toys. Paya has recently re-made several penny toy fire engines which are based on the pre-First World War toys by Meier (see **207–210**). Undoubtedly a wide range of penny toys was made by Paya, Rico and probably other Spanish manufacturers. They were not widely exported and are not well known outside Spain.

173 B 115 mm

174 C 100 mm

175 C 115 mm

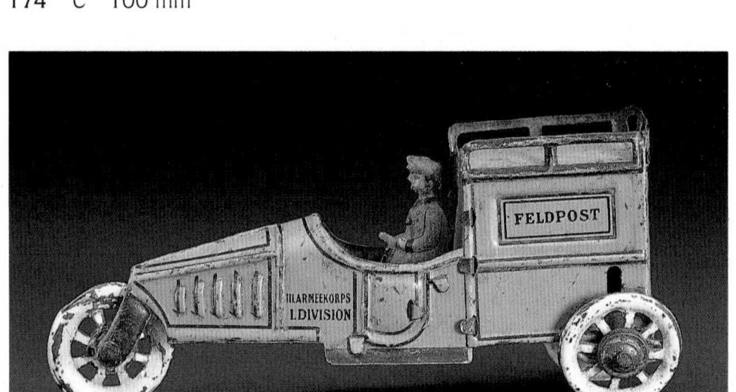

176 C 115 mm

177 C 115 mm

174, 175 A field kitchen and mounted gun by Meier. These toys were first produced shortly before 1914 and are typical of the type of penny toys which were to be produced in the early war years.

176, 177 Lithographic variants of a motorized tricycle. Both probably by Distler.

178 C 100 mm

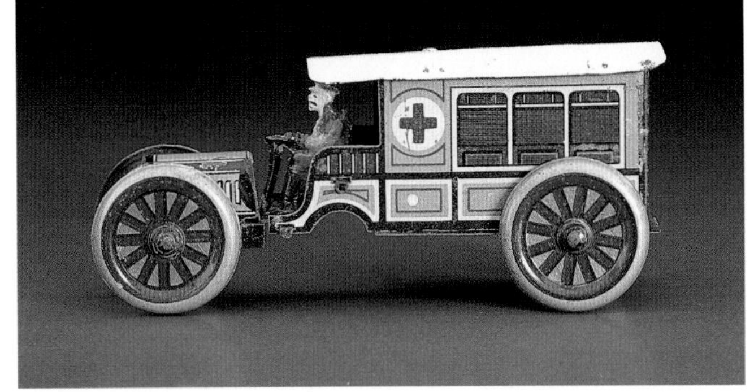

179 C 100 mm

180 B 75 mm

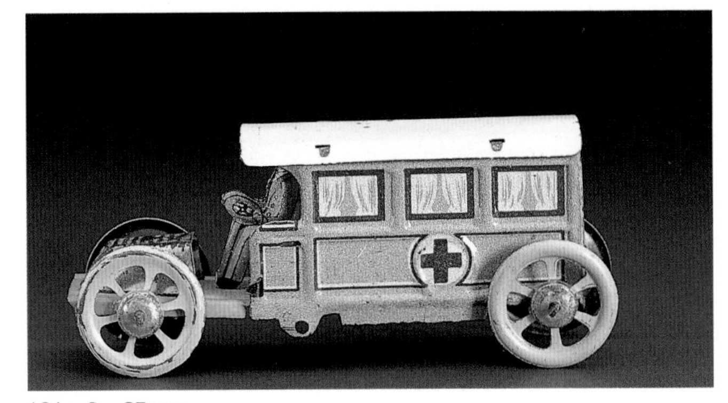

181 C 85 mm

178, 179 These two penny toys may have been sold individually but I have only seen them as part of a boxed set with soldiers. The box lid label has the JB trademark of Josef Bischoff of Nuremberg (a lead soldier maker) but Hess is the most likely manufacturer as the wheels and lithography are so typical.

180 A typical First World War armoured car made by Distler.

181 This ambulance was made by Meier and came in several different forms, both motorized and horsedrawn.

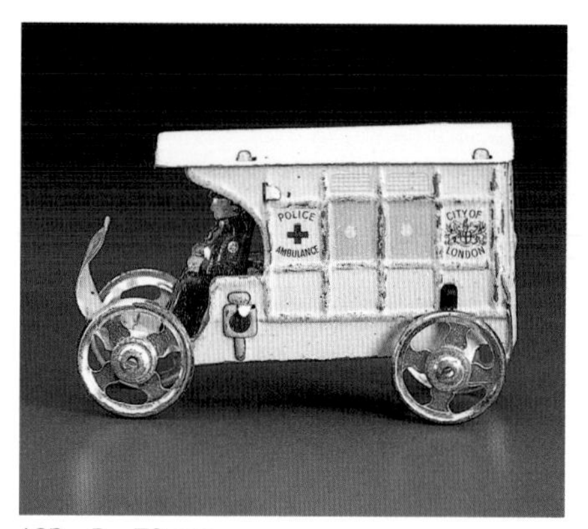

182 B 70 mm

183 B 70 mm

182 This City of London police Ambulance is a superb early Fischer penny toy, perhaps based on a curved dash Oldsmobile.

183 A wagonnette whose maker has not been identified.

184 A 75 mm

Detail of **182**

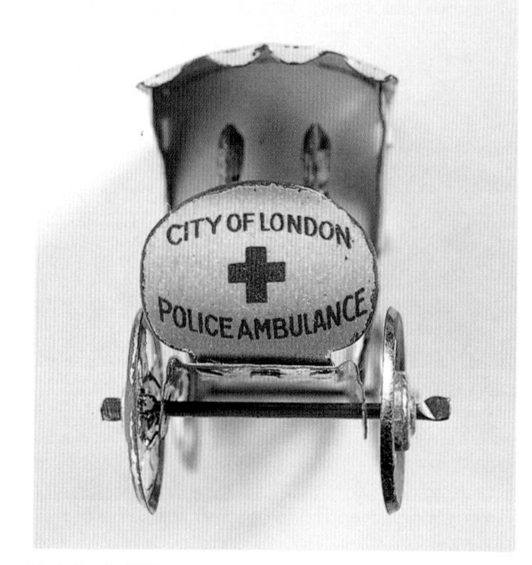

Detail of **182**

184 The bonnet section is identical to that found on several early Distler cars. The bodywork is unusual being a Postes et Télégraphes van for the French market. The wheels have lead hubs (typical of Meier) but are different to any other I have seen. It is impossible to be more specific as to the maker.

185 C 80 mm

186 C 80 mm

187 B 100 mm

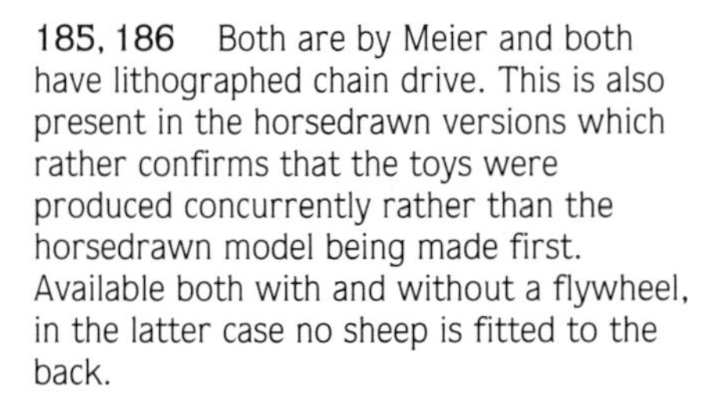

185, 186 Both are by Meier and both have lithographed chain drive. This is also present in the horsedrawn versions which rather confirms that the toys were produced concurrently rather than the horsedrawn model being made first. Available both with and without a flywheel, in the latter case no sheep is fitted to the back.

187 Probably made by Fischer.

188 D 95 mm

189 D 115 mm

190 B 95 mm

Three trucks by Fischer (**188**), Distler (**189**), and Issmayer (**190**). The Distler truck was also available with an arched canopy and Meier made a very similarly styled truck.

191 C 90 mm

192 D 100 mm

193 C 105 mm

191, 192 Both were made by G Fischer.

193 Petrol tankers or water tankers are unusual subjects for penny toy makers. This one is probably by Hess.

194 C 95 mm

195 C 90 mm

196 C 90 mm

A group of seven trucks by Distler all made both before 1914 and again in the 1920s. In the 1925 *Universal Toy Catalogue* most of these are also shown as being made in a horsedrawn version. I have yet to see one of these. They are either rare or possibly were not made. The optional kangaroo driver is shown in the covered wagon. The trucks with the sliding removable gold tops to the bonnets pre-date those with the plain red bonnets. The exact change over date is impossible to determine but the early 1920s would be a reasonable guess.

197 C 90 mm

198 C 80 mm

199 C 90 mm

200 C 92 mm

201 B 82 mm

202 B 80 mm

201 A beautifully detailed toy by Meier which evokes the charm of penny toys as well as any other. It is remarkable that so much care and attention to detail went into an object that was designed to retail for a penny. This toy optionally came with a sliding lid that sealed part of the upper deck and thereby provided a sweet container.

202 A well-detailed omnibus for the London market made by Fischer.

Details of **201**

203 C 90 mm

204 C 115 mm

205 C 105 mm

206 B 100 mm

The two general omnibuses (**203**, **204**) were made by Fischer. Kico was responsible for **206** which optionally came with a clockwork mechanism. Distler is the most likely manufacturer of the fourth bus. (**205**)

207 B 85 mm

208 C 85 mm

209 C 85 mm

210 C 85 mm

Four Meier fire toys which were first made before 1914 and which form a decorative set. I have always considered the hose reel wagon to be the rarest of these four. All four were illustrated in the 1924 *Universal Toy Catalogue*.

211 B 75 mm

212 B 70 mm

213 C 80 mm

214 C 100 mm

211, 212 Both probably made by Fischer. These fire engines were sold in a boxed set along with the semi-flat series of figures used in several of the photographs of penny toy fire equipment.

213, 214 Long and short wheelbase versions of a fire pumper by Distler.

215 A 85 mm

215 In the same series as **211** and **212** illustrated on the previous page, this toy is probably by Fischer. The lithographed firemen sitting on each side at the back without any embossing are particularly well printed.

216, 217 Both toys were made by Georg Fischer.

216 B 90 mm

217 B 90 mm

218 D 110 mm

219 D 125 mm

220 D 95 mm

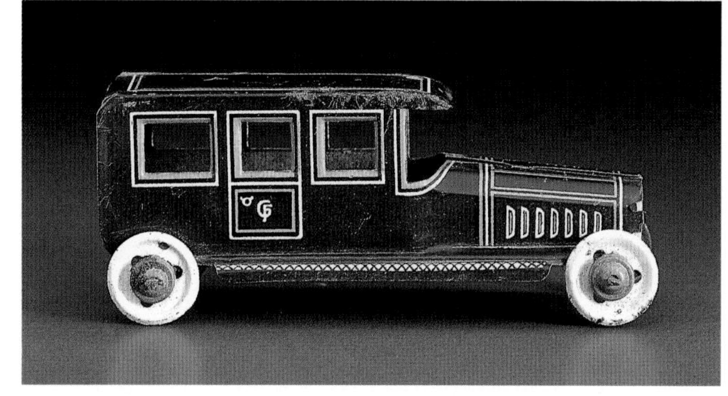

221 D 85 mm

All four cars were made by Georg Fischer and date from the 1920s and 1930s. Most penny toys of this period had lost their earlier charm and were rather bland in appearance.

222 D 100 mm

223 D 100 mm

224 D 95 mm

225 C 100 mm

Detail of **225**

222, 223 Two rather plain saloon cars by Fischer. They both have the same body pressings, differing only in their lithography.

224 Made by Kellermann in the 1920s.

225 The figures in the windows and bright colours help to enhance this Distler saloon and make it more visually pleasing than cars of a similar period by Fischer and Meier.

226 C 90 mm

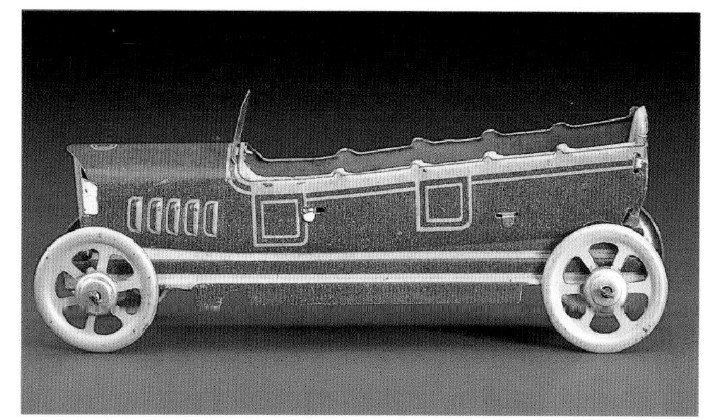

227 C 110 mm

228 C 80 mm

229 D 100 mm

226, 227 Both vehicles are by Meier. The red car with the flat military figure is the most atypical Meier penny toy that I have seen. The whole body section is pressed out of a single piece of tin; the driver is a separate flat pressing, the wheels are crude and the tinplate is of very poor quality. How are the mighty fallen! This toy must have made towards the end of Meier's production in 1934.

228 An attractively lithographed road roller which was probably made by Fischer.

229 A tractor by Distler which was sold either with or without a trailer.

230 B 105 mm

231 B 70 mm

232 B 85 mm

Detail of **231**

Three very interesting Japanese made penny toys from the 1920s or 1930s of which **230** and **231** were made by KS. Two (**230, 232**) whilst not being direct copies are similar in design to German penny toys. The most marked differences are the driver in **232** and the lithographed figures in the windows of **230** which are typically Japanese. The third car has virtually no affinity to any German made penny toy and it has an oriental charm of its own.

Japanese tin penny toys from the 1920s and 1930s are not common. These three are examples of the type of vehicles made. I am certain there are a great many more different models which could probably fill a book in their own right.

RAILWAY

233 A 90 mm

234 A 110 mm

235 C 85 mm

236 B 220 mm

233, 234 These are simple hand-painted German toy trains from the 1880s. The manufacturer has not been identified. They are the precursors of true penny toys.

235 Although illustrated in the 1901 Bing catalogue I think that the manufacturer was either Hess or less likely Issmayer. Small trains by both these makers feature in this catalogue. Compare plates **308–310**.

236 A hand-painted penny toy train that is strongly reminiscent of the larger scale floor trains made by Faivre in Paris. If not by Faivre, then this is certainly by one the other small makers who joined up in 1902 to form Jouets de Paris. Jouets de Paris continued to produce a wide range of penny toy type trains for several years after their inception. For further reading C Lamming's *JEP Le Jouet de Paris* is recommended.

237 A simple but charming boxed French penny toy train made by SMJ (Saint Mihiel Jeune). Although the style of train dates from the mid-nineteenth century this toy was probably made many years later. Very similar toys were made by JEP in their early years. The identification of this toy has only been made possible by the discovery of an original box and the help of the Musée des Arts Decoratifs in Paris.

238 Rossignol's little Train Express had a long production run. The delicate casting of the chimney, smoke and steam dome is made of tin.

239 Almost certainly an early JEP product.

237 C 170 mm

238 C 190 mm

239 C 157 mm

240 C 95 mm

241 D 105 mm

242 D 103 mm

These three make believe trains in which the locomotive and carriage are made as one have many similarities. **240** was made by Meier in the early years of this century, while **241** is a later and cruder example by the same manufacturer. **242** was made by Distler in the 1920s.

243 This ubiquitous small locomotive was made by Hess. It had a long production run.

244 An unusual penny toy being part locomotive and part road roller. There is an internal cog wheel reminiscent of Issmayer toys and this toy is possibly by that maker.

243 E 65 mm

244 C 75 mm

245 C 380 mm

245 Early examples of this toy, which was probably made by Hess, feature transfer printing on the carriages. The design was first printed on to thin paper and then stuck on the carriage. Later versions have the design lithographed directly onto the tinplate. The two versions are difficult to distinguish in a photograph.

246 C 90 mm

247 C 90 mm

248 C 104 mm

English, Continental and American versions of a similar penny toy. All three are by Meier.

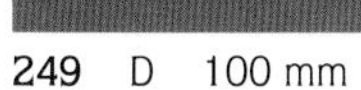

249 D 100 mm

250 C 80 mm

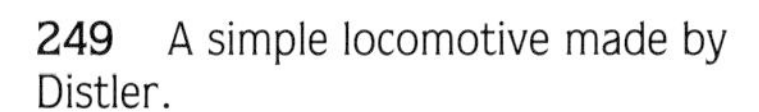

249 A simple locomotive made by Distler.

250 An Italian version dating from the 1920s of an earlier German penny toy.

251 I believe this toy to be by Distler but this is so far unconfirmed.

251 C 150 mm

252 C 250 mm

253 C 710 mm

254 C 300 mm

252 A simple freight train made by Kico which is enlivened by the tin smoke billowing out of the funnel.

253 This attractive Pennsylvania Limited train was produced in other American railway company liveries and came both with and without a clockwork mechanism. It is illustrated in the 1905 Carette catalogue but was probably manufactured by Hess or Issmayer.

254 Hess made many penny toy train sets in this style usually with bright lithography. It is possible that this slightly dull Great Northern Railway set was made by the firm of A Schuhmann rather than Hess.

255 An example of an attractive toy produced as a genuine penny toy train. Both Distler and Fischer made composite trains in this format in several different outlines and liveries. This example in Midland Railway livery can be attributed to Distler.

256 Probably by Hess.

257 A superbly lithographed and complex Central London Railway penny toy set. Made by either Issmayer or Hess.

255 C 510 mm

256 C 145 mm

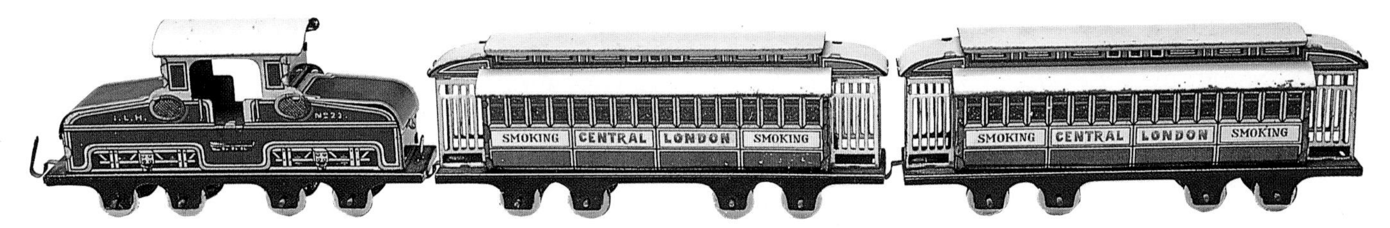

257 C 200 mm

258 A most attractive early Meier trolley with detailed embossing and lithography.

259 A single railway wagon by Meier.

258 B 80 mm

Details of **258**

259 C 92 mm

260 D 130 mm

261 C 120 mm

262 D 110 mm

263 C 115 mm

Four examples of Japanese penny toy trains very much in the style of Hess. Examples of Japanese trains of this type are frequently found but it is unusual to find two that are identical. Several different Japanese manufacturers exported them and each modified the lithography and style for different markets. Thus Great Eastern Railway (GER) was made for the British market and Pennsylvania Rail Road (PRR) was made for the US market.

264 Box lid

Most of the trains illustrated in this section are not true penny toys as they were frequently marketed as boxed sets with locomotive, carriages or wagons and cost considerably more than a penny. They were sold through the conventional retail trade. However the manufacturers frequently supplied via the wholesale trade and then street vendors sold individual components such as locomotives which would retail for a penny each. Sets could be sold with anything from one to a dozen wagons. The same locomotive might be offered at different prices with one, two, four or six carriages. It is impossible not to include these sets in any book on penny toys.

264, 265 This set was made in the 1920s and 1930s by Toyodo of Tokyo, Japan and came with twelve wagons and carriages. The colourful and exuberant design of the box lid label is typical of this era of Japanese graphics.

265 C 280 mm

DOLLS' HOUSE

266 A 80 mm

267 C 80 mm

268 C 74 mm

269 B 90 mm

266, 267 Both rocking chairs were made by Meier prior to 1914 and featured a compartment underneath which could be used as a candy container. The one containing the lithographed girl clutching her doll has infinitely more charm than the variation containing the Frozen Charlotte.

268 The bentwood rocking chair containing the boy with his rabbit was made by Meier in the pre-1914 era.

269 A simple rocking chair whose manufacturer has not been identified.

Detail of **266**

270 B 83 mm

271 B 95 mm

Detail of **271**

270 Although definitely of German origin, the maker of this baby carriage has not yet been identified. There are two slots in the coverlet which look as if they should hold something, but in all the examples seen by the author, this item has been absent.

271 This attractive baby carriage was made by Meier. It had a long production run from around 1905 to the late 1920s. No less than three variations of the Meier trademark are found on this one toy – the JM logo on the side, the embossed dog cart ventrally and an embossed M on the coverlet. A small sweet container tray could be fitted underneath.

272 C 90 mm

273 C 90 mm

Both toys were made by Fischer prior to 1914 and again in the 1920s. The carriage bodies not only feature different lithography but also were different pressings. Both prams contain a pivoting flat lithographed figure. At first glance these two figures appear identical but in reality they have many differences in dress. It will be left to the reader's own imagination as to why Fischer should put the figure of a young adult in these two prams!

Detail of **273**

274 The spirit-painted cast wheels would suggest that this is a French toy.

275 Many different items of dolls' house furniture were made of cast tin and sold either as bare metal or painted. Cast tin is a soft, malleable substance and is easily bent out of shape. This pram is an example of this type of toy and comes complete with its lace fittings.

276 A small brightly lithographed baby carriage made by Kellermann in the 1920s.

277 A small-scale pram by Fischer from the 1920s.

274 C 90 mm

275 C 55 mm

276 C 65 mm

277 C 70 mm

278 D 80 mm high

279 D 80 mm high

280 D 80 mm high

278–280 All are by Meier and are variations on the same toy. The sliding drawer (when fitted) could be used as a sweet container. These are common penny toys and this model in various guises had a long production run.

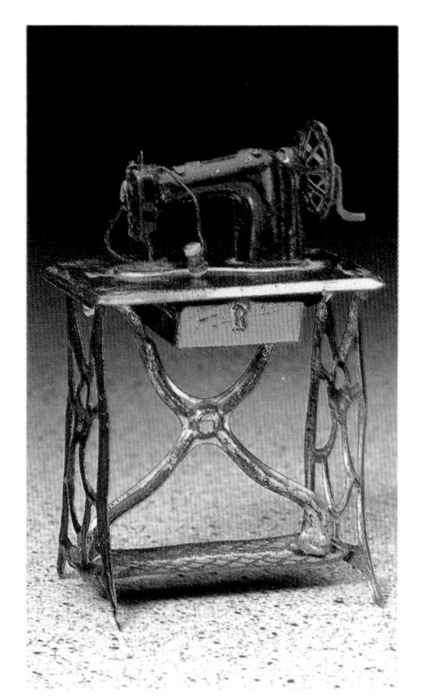

281 C 85 mm high

282 C 95 mm high

283 C 85 mm high

282 A slightly larger sewing machine by Fischer, dating from the 1920s.

281, 283 Both are attributable to the same maker who has not yet been identified.

284 C 43 mm

285 C 43 mm

284, 285 This school desk was made by Meier before 1914 and was available with either a seated boy or a girl. The desk top, which slides off to reveal a sweet compartment, was available with several different lithographed pictures.

The push chair (**287**) was probably made by Fischer, whereas the other chair (**286**) was definitely made by Distler.

286 C 70 mm

287 C 85 mm

288 D 100 mm high (extended)

289 C 90 mm high (extended)

290 C 45 mm

The three high chairs are remarkably similar but were made by three different manufacturers. Each could be used as a high chair or opened out to form a table and chair. Distler made the example illustrated in plate **291**, Meier the one in plate **289** and Fischer was probably the maker of that in plate **288**. The low chair on the right (**290**) is by Distler.

All four date from the 1920s but it is possible that they were made before 1914 as well.

291 D 100 mm high (extended)

292 C 75 mm high

293 D 85 mm high

292 A very high quality watering can, probably by Meier and dating from the turn of the century.

293 A tin globe on a stand made in the 1920s by an unidentified German maker.

294 An attractive phonograph by Meier which features a simple two note 'musical' movement.

295 A brightly lithographed coal scuttle that also acts as a money box. It is German made and dates from the early 1900s, but the manufacturer has not been identified.

294 C 90 mm

295 D 65 mm

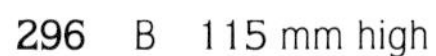

296 B 115 mm high

297 C 120 mm high

298 C 90 mm high

299 C 100 mm high

296 The bellows camera has a detachable lens cap and a photographic plate that was available with different images. Made by Meier in the pre-1914 era.

297 The elaborately lithographed telephone was produced by Meier prior to 1914.

298 A brightly lithographed parrot swings in the centre of this Meier cage. It was produced both before 1914 and again in the 1920s.

299 This simple hand-cranked steam plant was probably made by Distler.

300 C 65 mm high

301 D 75 mm

300 This vertical boiler was also sold as a whistle. It bears the unattributed monogram HD.

301 A commonly found penny toy, this canary cage was made by Meier for a long period. The canary pecks forward as the lever is pushed.

302 An early Meier milk cart.

303 This simple lithographed bird cage offers no clues as to its manufacturer. Probably German and dating from the late 1920s, it contains a minute, simple flat pressing of a canary.

302 D 110 mm

303 D 70 mm high

NAUTICAL

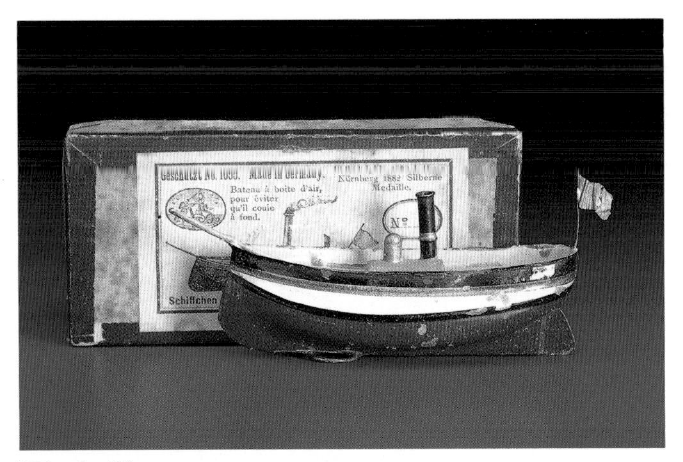

304 C 90 mm

305 B 80 mm

Without exception penny toy tin boats were floor running toys and were not designed to float at all. These four small boats are the precursors of true penny toys and were all designed to float. Many penny toy collectors however include a few examples in their collections.

306 C 70 mm

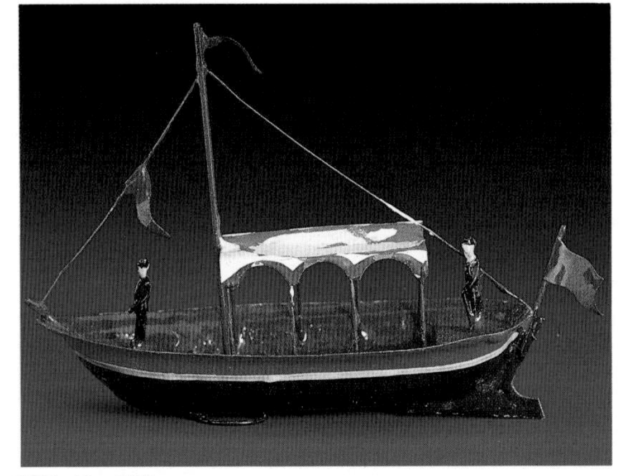

307 B 100 mm

304, 306 Boats of this type were made by both Uebelaker and Fleischmann in the late nineteenth century and in the early years of the twentieth century. They were always hand-painted, usually zinc hulled and nearly impossible to attribute unless found with their original box. Thus **304** is known to be by Uebelaker.

305, 307 Made mainly of brass and delicately hand-painted, these magnetic bath toys were made by Issmayer in the nineteenth century. Each had a small iron rod in its keel to enable it to be drawn along with a magnet.

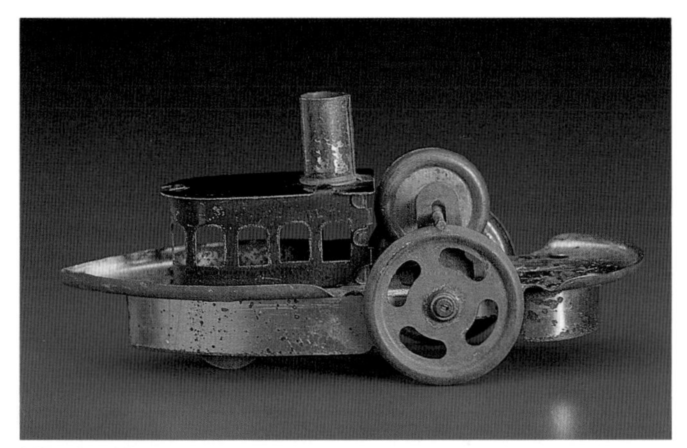

308 D 96 mm

309 D 96 mm

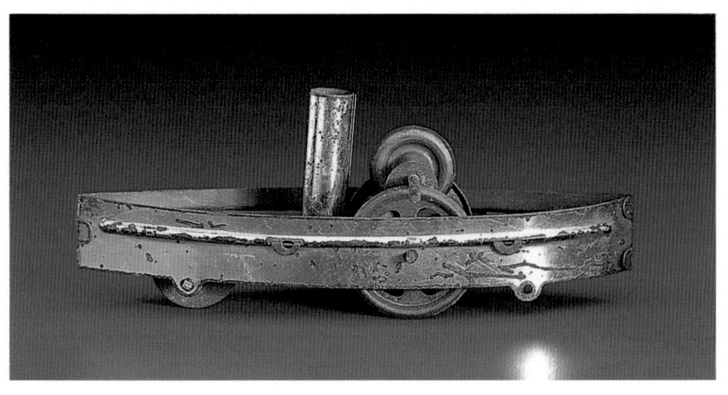

310 D 110 mm

311 D 115 mm

308, 309 Both are depicted in the 1901 Bing catalogue. Bing at this period sold toys made by other manufacturers. It is impossible to state categorically that Bing did not make these toys but there is strong evidence to suggest that they were made by Hess. **310** is not in the same catalogue but is certainly from the same source.

311 Made by Charles Rossignol of Paris.

312 C 105 mm

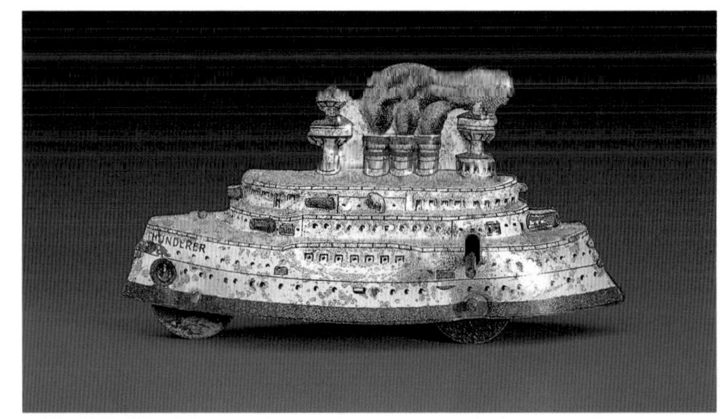

313 C 105 mm

314 C 100 mm

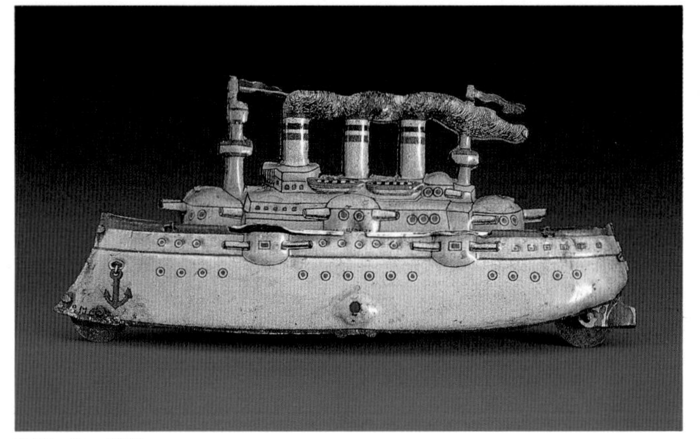

315 B 135 mm

312, 313 Thunderer and Indominatable are two lithographic variations of the same boat. There is no firm clue as to manufacturer except that the two simple side pressings with no base are reminiscent of Georg Fischer's series of flat and rather simple automobiles.

314, 315 Both are by Meier and are really size variants of the same boat.

316 C 125 mm

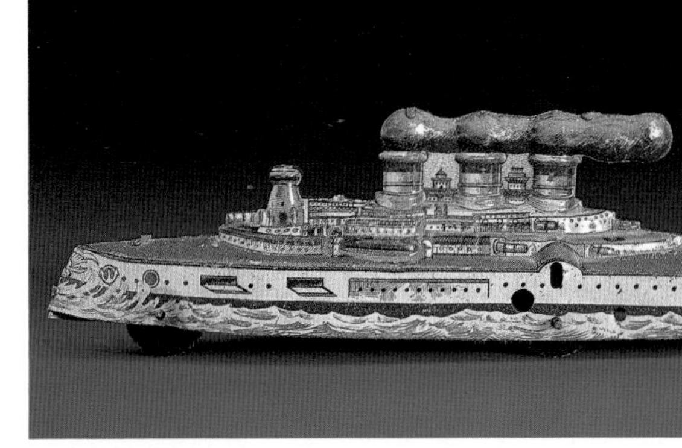

317 C 160 mm

318 C 120 mm

319 C 120 mm

316 A 1920s penny toy made by Distler. It was available with clockwork.

317 A similar style of battleship by Distler in a larger size and one which is on the borderline between being a penny toy and an ordinary tin toy.

318, 319 Both were made by Distler and use the same hull pressings to produce two very different boats.

320 C 75 mm

321 C 75 mm

Two of Meler's most attractive penny toys that although not rare are very desirable. The toys feature two of the wheel types used by Meier from about 1905 onwards.

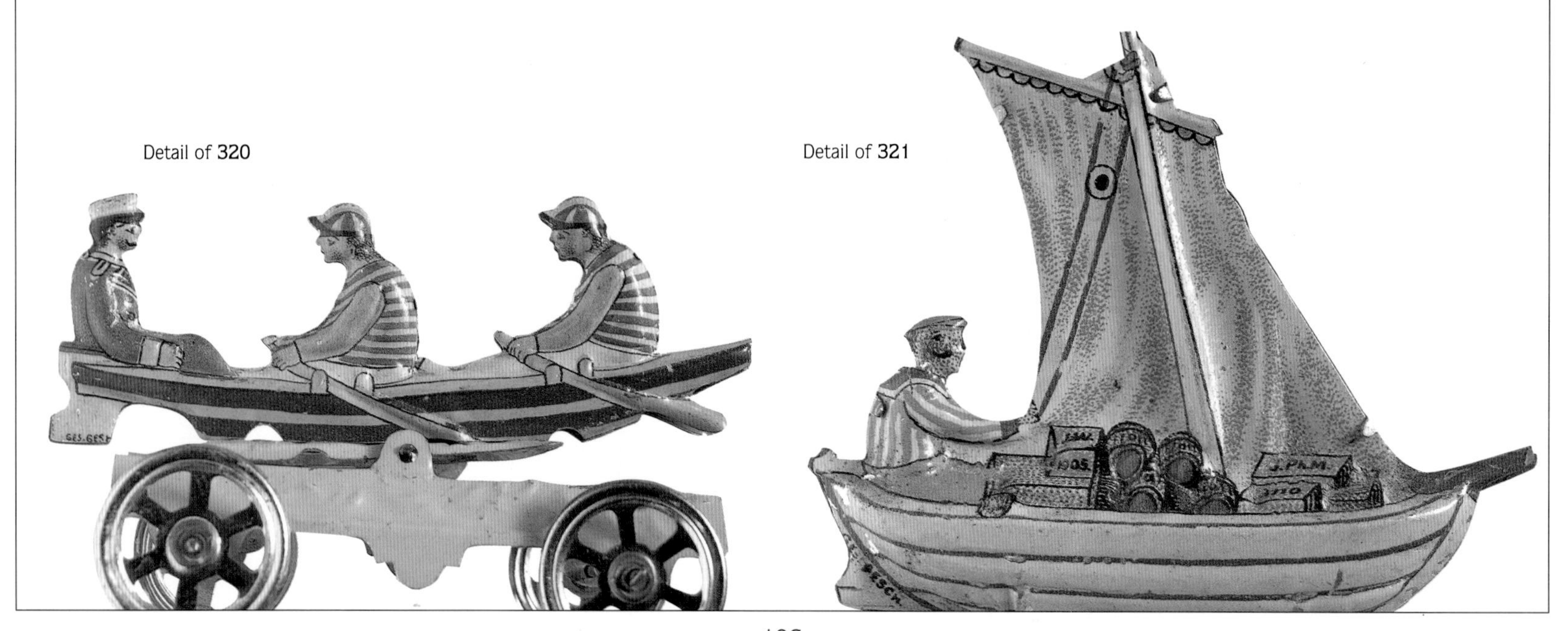

Detail of **320**

Detail of **321**

Three more of Meier's best penny toys. Meteor is not missing the forward cabin – this was the way this variation was shown in a catalogue illustration.

322 B 75 mm

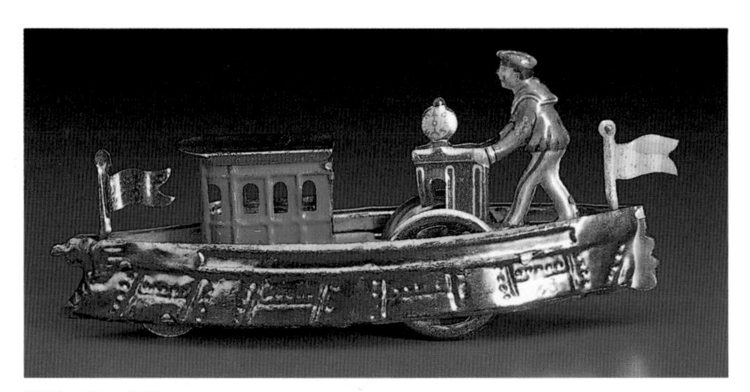

323 C 120 mm

324 C 120 mm

Detail of **322**

325 B 112 mm

326 B 112 mm

327 B 98 mm

325–327 All three were almost certainly made by Georg Fischer. They are attractive, well finished, early penny toys. The funnel of the gun boat doubles as a whistle.

328 B 107 mm

328 Made by Meier in the pre-1905 period. Although not trademarked, the embossed deck and hull are typical of the detail found in early Meier penny toys. The flags are identical to those found on other Meier boats, thus confirming its attribution. It is depicted in the 1901 Stollwerk catalogue. The front torpedo tube could be used as a gun to fire cachous or small peas.

Detail of **327**

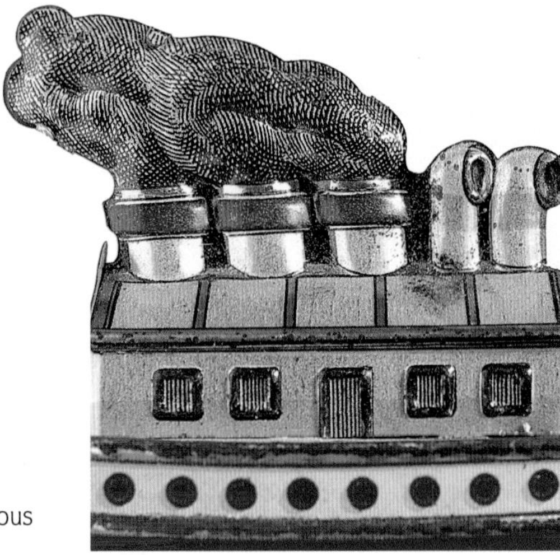

329 C 120 mm

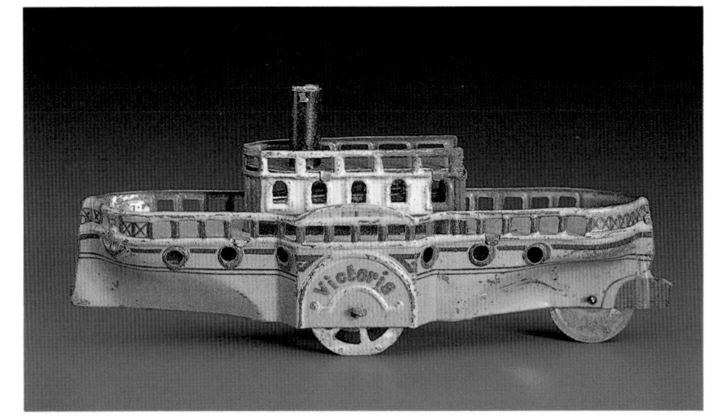

330 B 120 mm

331 D 115 mm

332 D 110 mm

Four attractive passenger boats that had long production runs. The four depicted are almost certainly pre-1914 examples, as 1920s models were simplified. I have seen a late Victoria painted entirely green and looking very drab compared with its colourful forbear. **329** is by Distler, **331** by Meier, **332** by Fischer and **330** probably by Meier.

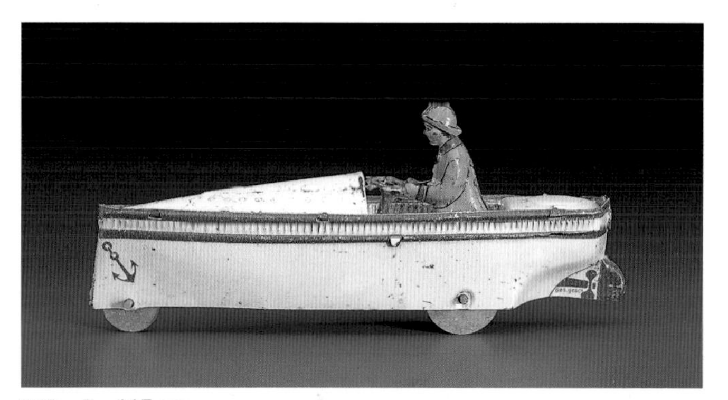

333 B 115 mm

334 E 120 mm

335 B 175 mm

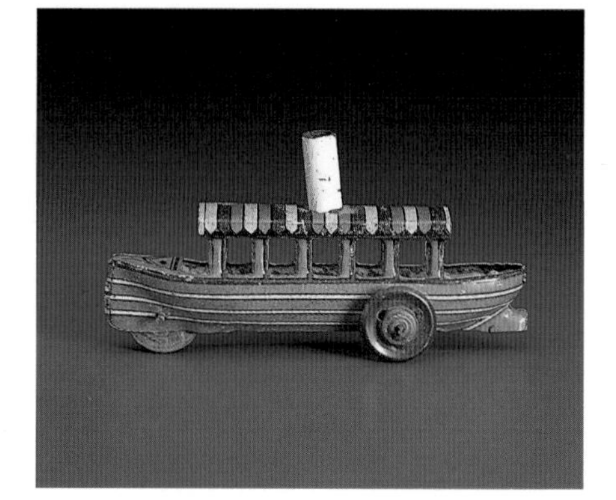

336 D 80 mm

333 The speedboat by Meier is interesting in that it contains a lady driver.

334 Many different small mechanical toy boats were made featuring one, two or four rowers by such makers as Kellermann and Levy. Generally these are just beyond the scale of true penny toys. This example was made by Levy as a promotional sales or give away item for UTCC in Chicago.

335 A large non-mechanical penny toy which by the evidence of holes cut in the hull was also available with clockwork. The manufacturer has not yet been identified.

336 This small toy was made by Fischer in the 1920s. A very similar toy but with a covered paddlebox was made in the same era by Meier.

BANKS, BUILDINGS & CANDY CONTAINERS

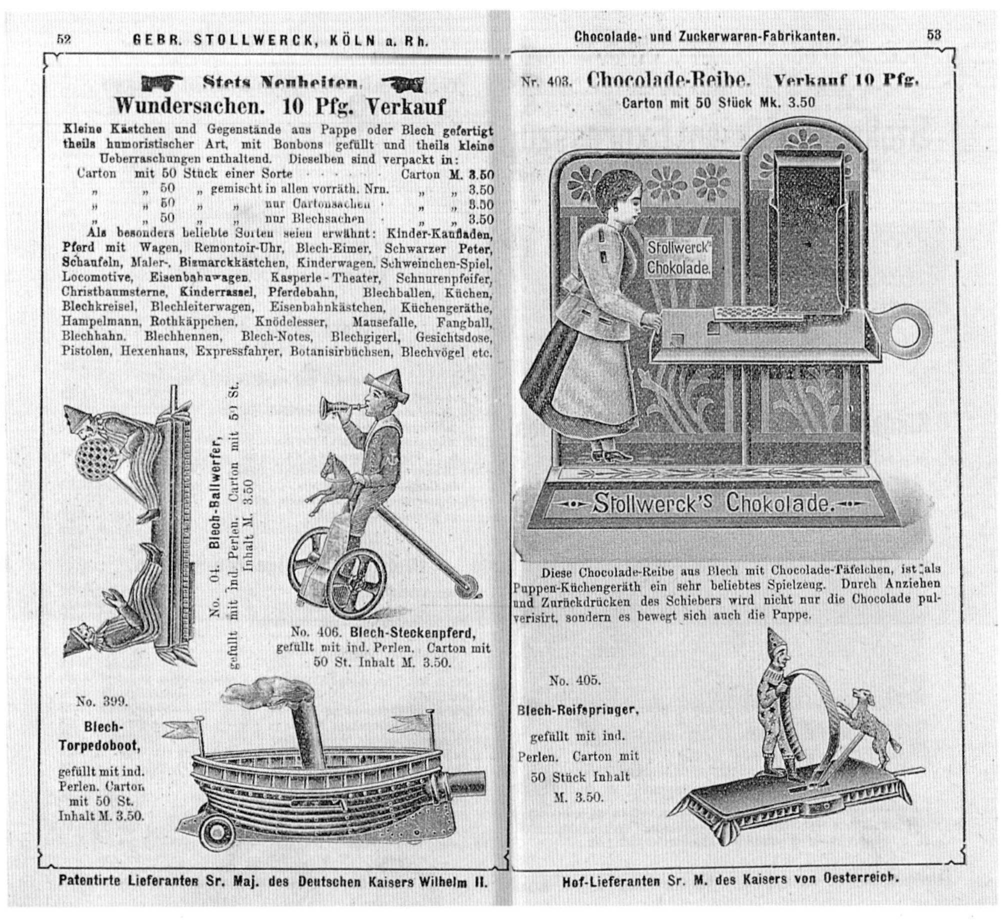

52 GEBR. STOLLWERCK, KÖLN a. Rh.

Stets Neuheiten.

Wundersachen. 10 Pfg. Verkauf

Kleine Kästchen und Gegenstände aus Pappe oder Blech gefertigt theils humoristischer Art, mit Bonbons gefüllt und theils kleine Ueberraschungen enthaltend. Dieselben sind verpackt in:

Carton mit 50 Stück einer Sorte · · · Carton M. 3.50
" " 50 " gemischt in allen vorräth. Nrn. " " 3.50
" " 50 " " nur Cartonsachen · " " 3.50
" " 50 " " nur Blechsachen · " " 3.50

Als besonders beliebte Sorten seien erwähnt: Kinder-Kaufladen, Pferd mit Wagen, Remontoir-Uhr, Blech-Eimer, Schwarzer Peter, Schaufeln, Maler-, Bismarckkästchen, Kinderwagen, Schweinchen-Spiel, Locomotive, Eisenbahnwagen, Kasperle-Theater, Schnurenpfeifer, Christbaumsterne, Kinderrassel, Pferdebahn, Blechballen, Küchen, Blechkreisel, Blechleiterwagen, Eisenbahnkästchen, Küchengeräthe, Hampelmann, Rothkäppchen, Knödelesser, Mausefalle, Fangball, Blechhahn, Blechhennen, Blech-Notes, Blechgigerl, Gesichtsdose, Pistolen, Hexenhaus, Expressfahrer, Botanisirbüchsen, Blechvögel etc.

No. 04. **Blech-Ballwerfer,** gefüllt mit ind. Perlen. Carton mit 50 St. Inhalt M. 3.50.

No. 406. **Blech-Steckenpferd,** gefüllt mit ind. Perlen. Carton mit 50 St. Inhalt M. 3.50.

No. 399. **Blech-Torpedoboot,** gefüllt mit ind. Perlen. Carton mit 50 St. Inhalt M. 3.50.

Patentirte Lieferanten Sr. Maj. des Deutschen Kaisers Wilhelm II.

Chocolade- und Zuckerwaren-Fabrikanten. 53

Nr. 403. **Chocolade-Reibe. Verkauf 10 Pfg.**

Carton mit 50 Stück Mk. 3.50

Diese Chocolade-Reibe aus Blech mit Chocolade-Täfelchen, ist als Puppen-Küchengeräth ein sehr beliebtes Spielzeug. Durch Anziehen und Zurückdrücken des Schiebers wird nicht nur die Chocolade pulverisirt, sondern es bewegt sich auch die Puppe.

No. 405. **Blech-Reifspringer,** gefüllt mit ind. Perlen. Carton mit 50 Stück Inhalt M. 3.50.

Hof-Lieferanten Sr. M. des Kaisers von Oesterreich.

337 Stollwerck Christmas catalogue

337 A double page taken from the Stollwerck of Cologne catalogue for Christmas 1901 which clearly shows that many well known penny toys could be very simply modified to become candy containers. Indeed, it is my opinion that most pre-1914 penny toys could be used and sold as candy containers. This was done in the case of the mechanical novelty toys by the fitting of a tray underneath (as in the two clowns), or by closing a compartment with a sliding lid (as in the top floor of a double decker bus). The list of penny toys that Stollwerck used is quite extensive. All those pictured were made by Meier.

(Right) Four simple carts, whose maker has not been identified, all of which had sliding lids and could be sold filled with sweets.

338 C 95 mm

339 B 95 mm

340 C 95 mm

341 C 95 mm

342 A 90 mm high

343 A 95 mm high

344 C 95 mm high

342, 343 The hare and bear both have compartments in their bases for sweets. The hare incorporates a whistle and the bear plays his cymbals. Both are of high quality, certainly German made, but have a different feel and method of construction to other penny toys. The manufacturer has not been identified, but could be a tin maker rather than a traditional toy maker. A bear incorporating a whistle and a lion which dispenses cachous through the mouth are also known.

344 A Meier devotional penny toy that could be pinned onto a bedroom wall. The altar cloth slides off to reveal a sweet compartment.

345 A beautifully detailed and intricate mechanical dispenser by Fischer. The chicken will actually lay a small sweet with each rotation of the rear wheels as she is pushed along.

346 The chicken on the basket also has a sweet-laying mechanism. It is marked GMS underneath. Almost certainly German in origin, the manufacturer has not been identified. I have seen other toys on a similar basket base.

345 B 75 mm

346 B 55 mm

Details of **345**

347 C 80 mm high

348 B 90 mm high

347 This penny toy vending machine has compartments to dispense two different kinds of sweets. The maker has not been identified.

348 The high quality embossed tin and typical colour would suggest that this dispenser in the form of a fountain was made by Meier in the 1890s.

349, 350 Both are candy firing guns. **350** has the advantage of a target and a candy container with a sliding lid. The manufacturer of this toy was HMN (see **45, 46**). The red cannon was made by Meier.

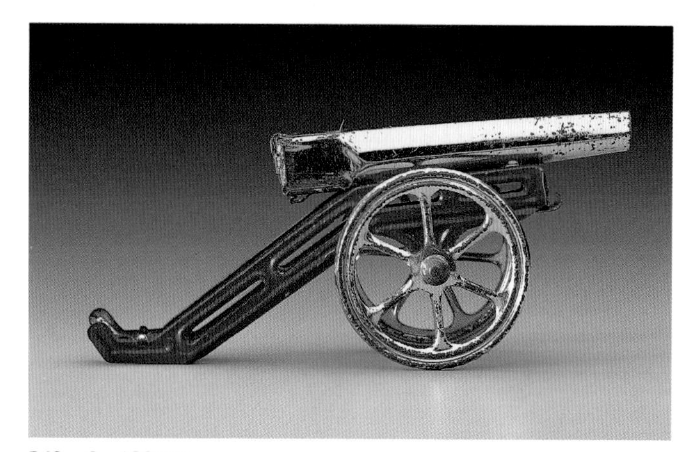

349 C 120 mm

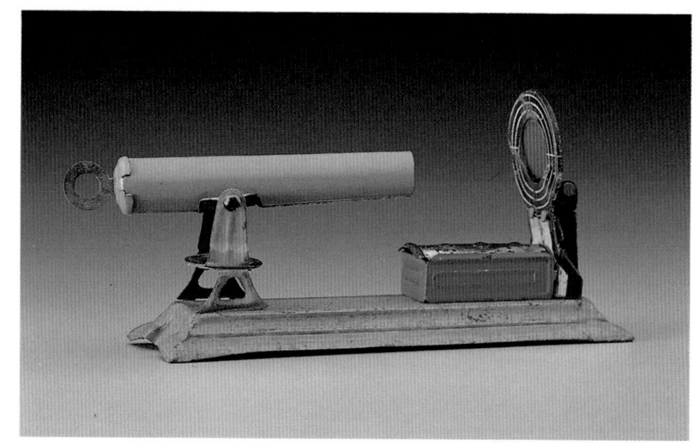

350 B 100 mm

351 D 90 mm high

352 B 85 mm high

353 B 90 mm high

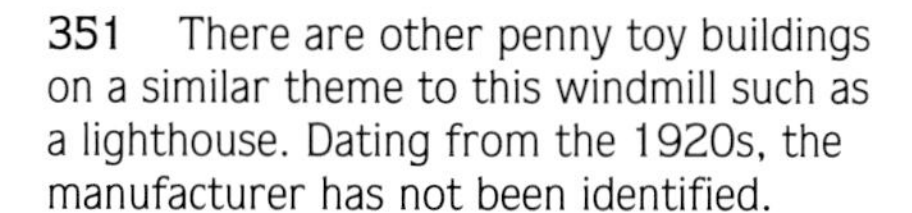

351 There are other penny toy buildings on a similar theme to this windmill such as a lighthouse. Dating from the 1920s, the manufacturer has not been identified.

352 The perpetual calendar consists of three rotating card discs behind the facade of a gothic clock tower. The high quality lithography would suggest a pre-1914 manufacturing date. The maker is unknown.

353 The weighted roly-poly clown has a sweet container in the base. Unknown maker.

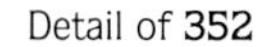

Detail of **352**

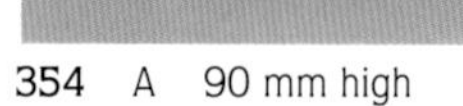

354 A 90 mm high

355 A 90 mm high

354, 355 Top quality Meier lithography make these two animated candy dispensers irresistable. The fairy stories of Little Red Riding Hood and Cinderella are easily recognizable. When the lever at the side is depressed the picture in the window changes and a sweet is dispensed. A third dispenser of the Hansel and Gretel gingerbread house is also known.

Detail of **355**

356 C 70 mm high

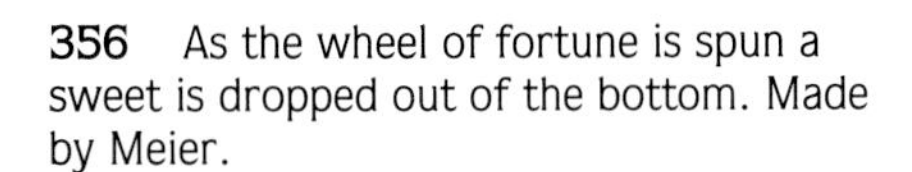
356 As the wheel of fortune is spun a sweet is dropped out of the bottom. Made by Meier.

357 When the lever is depressed the child's expression changes from sad to happy and a sweet is dispensed. Maker unknown, but the base plate is very similar to that of the perpetual calendar (**352**) suggesting they have the same origins.

357 C 90 mm high

358 D 70 mm

359 C 63 mm

360 C 63 mm

These seven penny toys are examples of the many different types of buildings that were made into banks. They are all non-mechanical and their main interest lies in the quality of lithography. All have a slot in the top through which the coin is inserted and most have a locking and hinged roof to permit removal of the savings. All seven are of German origin although their makers have not been identified.

361 D 63 mm

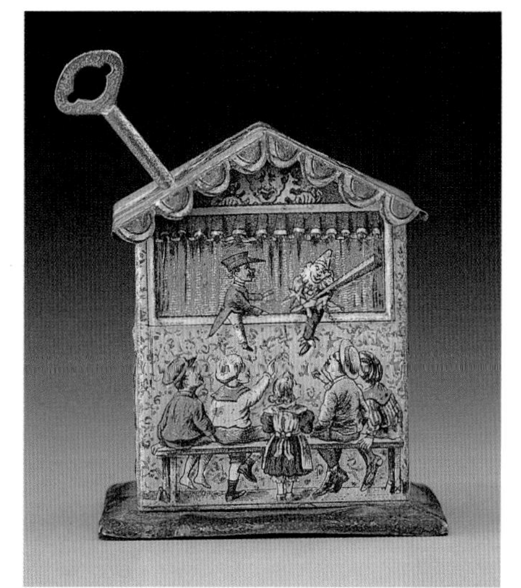
362 C 70 mm high

363 C 70 mm high

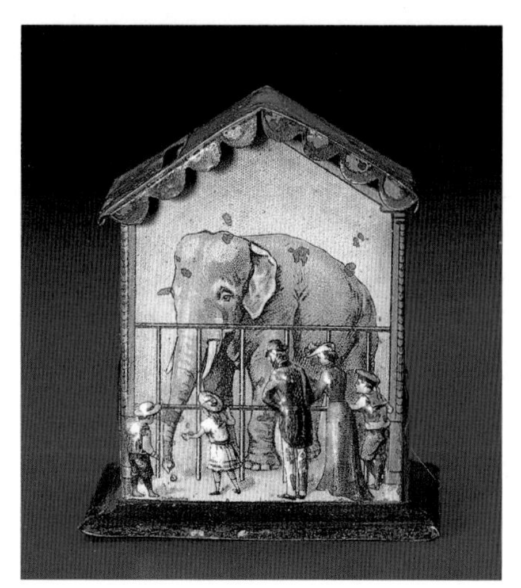
364 C 70 mm high

365 B–C 82–95 mm

The production of beautifully lithographed tin containers was an area in which the British excelled and for many years collectors have admired the range of miniature tins by Rowntree, Pascall, Clarnico and other sweet manufacturers without always realizing their true origins, or the fact that they could be considered as penny toys. Marguerite Fawdry, during research for her book *British Tin Toys* was shown a list of 'penny novelties' made by Barringer, Wallis and Manners of Mansfield, Staffordshire. This well-known firm of tin makers was absorbed into the Metal Box company empire in 1939 and it is in their archives that this list was found. The list of over 40 'penny novelties' contained many of the Rowntrees miniature tins, as well as items made for Pascall's, Clarnico and Batger's. This evidence would suggest that Barringer, Wallis and Manners were the makers of the majority of English penny sweet containers.

Almost all these are static cachou containers, their attraction lying in the quality of lithography. However, Barringer, Wallis and Manners did make a Punch and Judy booth for Rowntrees in which the figure of Punch moves. Some of these sweet containers are found in the King collection suggesting that they were sold by street vendors as well as retail shops. A Rowntrees cricket bat promoting a Dick Whittington pantomime has also been recorded.

Of the six items illustrated, all are Rowntree except the Scotsman who is unmarked, but may have been made by Barringer, Wallis and Manners for Pascall. These miniature tins were primarily sold in the 1900–1914 era, although it is likely that some production continued after the First World War.

WHISTLES

366 E 110 mm

(page 123)
Twelve colourful Japanese made tin whistles which were primarily cracker toys from the 1920s and 1930s. It is quite possible that they were sold individually as penny toys. The individual makers are not known.

366–371 A group of six whistles which when blown not only emit a sound but also have a spinning feature. The grindstones, carrousel, squirrel cage, wheel of fortune and poodle are the respective spinning elements. All date from the 1920s.

366 and **368** are by unknown French manufacturers. **367** was made by Kico. **369** and **370** are marked E C France. **371** is probably attributable to Distler.

367 C 105 mm

368 D 105 mm

369 D 85 mm

370 C 105 mm

371 D 110 mm

372 B 110 mm

373 B 107 mm

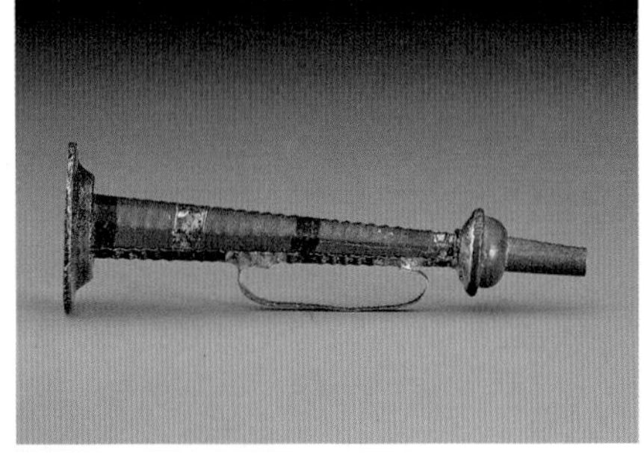

374 D 95 mm

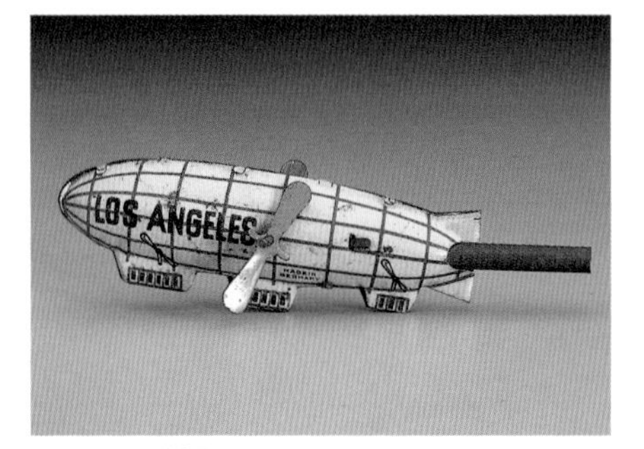

375 D 105 mm

376 D 90 mm

372 A delightful penny whistle that mimics the sound of a cock crowing. It is German made and dates from the late nineteenth century.

373 An elaborate whistle that features a cast tin lady stepping out of a mill. Probably German.

374 The classic penny whistle in the form of a conical trumpet. It has hand soldered seams. This is the type of toy assembled by a family of home workers in Germany at the turn of the century.

375 Dating from the 1920s, this airship is of German manufacture.

376 A simple German penny whistle in the shape of a horn. Such items were made by several manufacturers, both before and after the First World War.

FANTASY

377 B 80 mm

378 C 100 mm

379 C 100 mm

380 C 100 mm

Four classic Meier mechanical penny toys initially made in the first decade of this century. All had long production runs and were still available in the 1920s. However, the brilliance and clarity of the lithography had greatly diminished by then.

381 C 80 mm

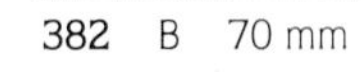

382 B 70 mm

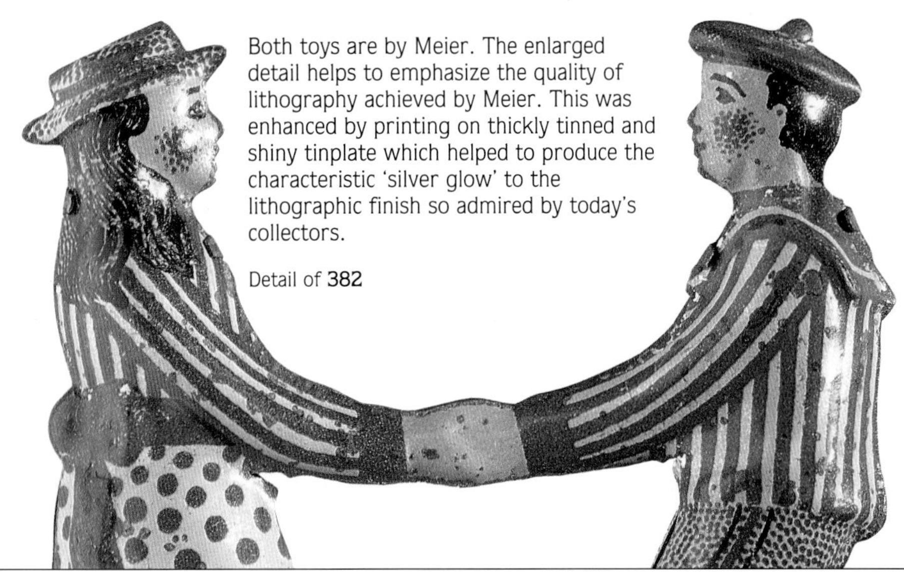

Both toys are by Meier. The enlarged detail helps to emphasize the quality of lithography achieved by Meier. This was enhanced by printing on thickly tinned and shiny tinplate which helped to produce the characteristic 'silver glow' to the lithographic finish so admired by today's collectors.

Detail of **382**

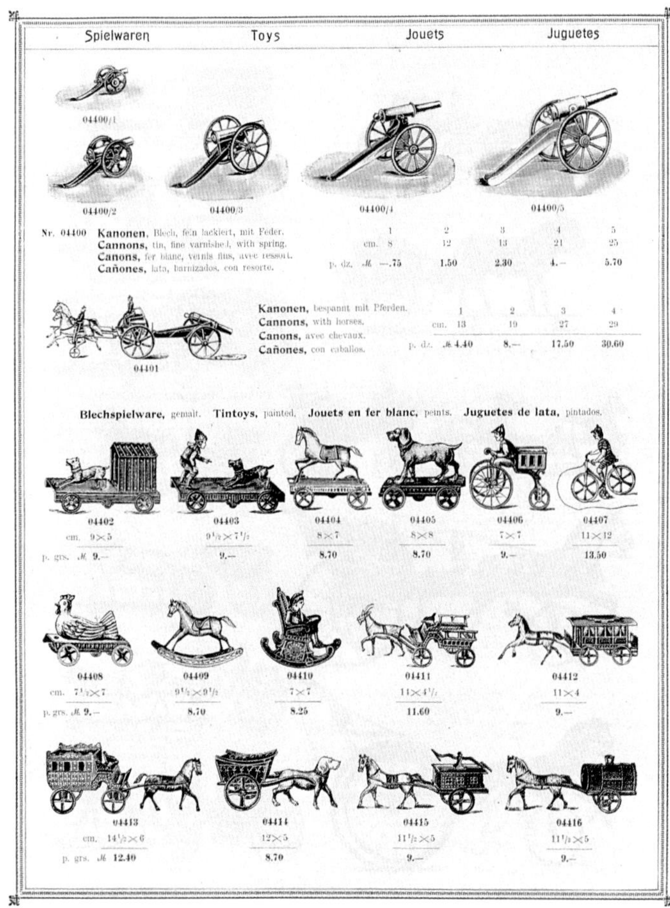

Spielwaren	Toys	Jouets	Juguetes

04400/1 04400/2 04400/3 04400/4 04400/5

Nr. 04400	**Kanonen,** Blech, fein lackiert, mit Feder. **Cannons,** tin, fine varnished, with spring. **Canons,** fer blanc, vernis fins, avec ressort. **Cañones,** lata, barnizados, con resorte.	1	2	3	4	5
	cm.	8	12	13	21	25
	p. dz. ℳ	–.75	1.50	2.30	4.–	5.70

04401	**Kanonen,** bespannt mit Pferden. **Cannons,** with horses. **Canons,** avec chevaux. **Cañones,** con caballos.	1	2	3	4
	cm.	13	19	27	29
	p. dz. ℳ	4.40	8.–	17.50	30.60

Blechspielware, gemalt. **Tintoys,** painted. **Jouets en fer blanc,** peints. **Juguetes de lata,** pintados.

	04402	04403	04404	04405	04406	04407
cm.	9×5	9½×7½	8×7	8×8	7×7	11×12
p. grs. ℳ	9.–	9.–	8.70	8.70	9.–	13.50

	04408	04409	04410	04411	04412
cm.	7½×7	9½×9½	7×7	11×4½	11×4
p. grs. ℳ	9.–	8.70	8.25	11.60	9.–

	04413	04414	04415	04416
cm.	14½×6	12×5	11½×5	11½×5
p. grs. ℳ	12.40	8.70	9.–	9.–

383 1900 catalogue

Blechspielwaren farbig bemalt.
Tintoys colored.
Jouets en fer blanc colorés.
Juguetes de lata colorados.

Verpackung lose in Cartons à 2 dz.
Packing loose in boxes à 2 doz.
Emballage en vrac en cartons de 2 douz.
Embalaje en cartones de 2 doz.

384 1909 catalogue

383 Shows a page from the wholesaler Ullman and Engelmann's catalogue from about 1900. It features several of Meier's earliest penny toys. Some are all spirit-painted while others are partially lithographed.

384 Shows a page from Ullmann and Engelmann's catalogue of circa 1909. It features many of Meier's classic penny toys.

385 B 90 mm

386 B 77 mm

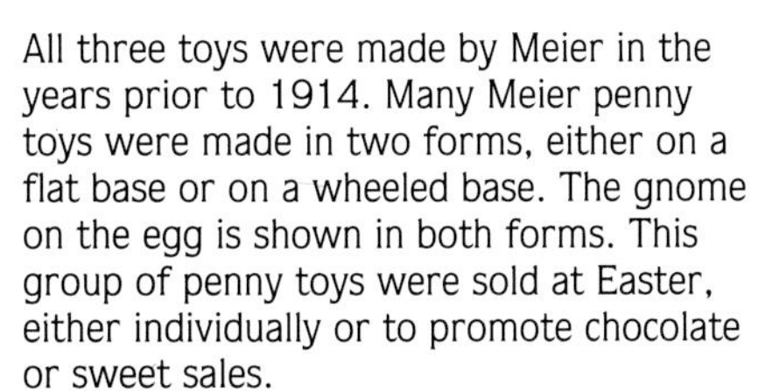

All three toys were made by Meier in the years prior to 1914. Many Meier penny toys were made in two forms, either on a flat base or on a wheeled base. The gnome on the egg is shown in both forms. This group of penny toys were sold at Easter, either individually or to promote chocolate or sweet sales.

387 B 70 mm

Detail of **385**

388 A 100 mm

389 C 100 mm

390 C 100 mm

391 C 100 mm

All four toys were made by Meier. The toys of the gnomes and the girl feeding the chicken were first produced about 1902 but were still available in the 1920s. The two examples of gnomes are commonly found on a wheeled base.

392 A 95 mm

393 B 80 mm

394 B 90 mm

395 B 82 mm

Four Meier toys. **392** is of particular note as it is all painted rather than lithographed. This is typical of Meier's early penny toy production. Lithography was gradually introduced around 1900, enabling a better and more detailed finish to be achieved and eliminating the painting stage.

396 A 100 mm

397 A 100 mm

398 B 100 mm

A group of three mechanical penny toys by Meier depicting the sporting images of soccer, boxing and lawn tennis. All three are rare and desirable.

Both these Meier penny toys could double as candy containers. The Father Christmas toy has a sliding top to the sleigh and the sweep and boy penny toy was sold with a sliding tray that ran in a groove on the base, thus fitting neatly above the axles.

399 A 65 mm

Detail of **399**

400 A 100 mm

Detail of **400**

401 B 67 mm

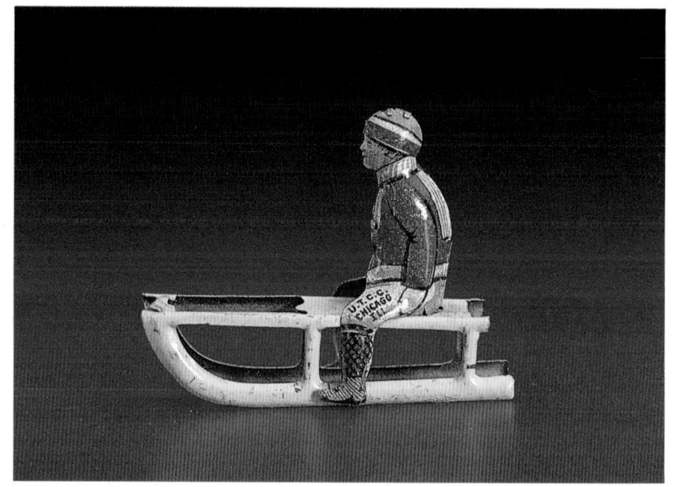

402 C 65 mm

403 C 77 mm

An interesting group of penny toys that reflect the growing interest in winter sports during the 1920s. The two toys marked UTCC (Universal Theatres Concession Company of Chicago Illinois) were promotional items. **401** is by Distler, **402** and **403** are probably by G Levy (marked UTCC) and **404–406** are by Meier.

404 C 95 mm

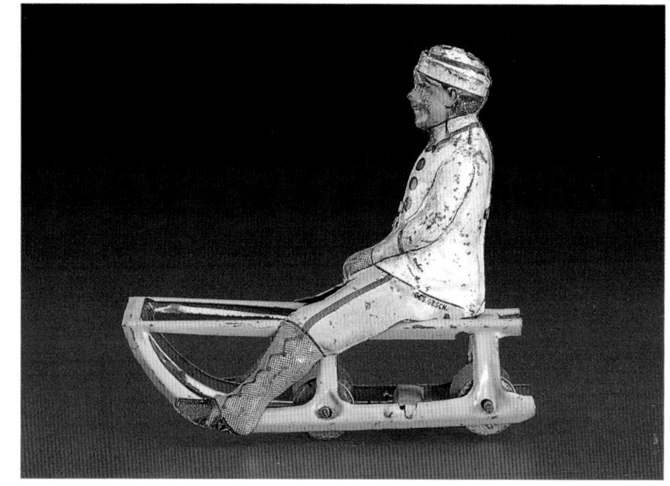

405 C 75 mm

406 C 88 mm

407 A 90 mm

408 A 92 mm

Detail of **408**

Detail of **407**

The boy dressed in a sailor suit riding a hobby horse is an early Meier penny toy. The system whereby the four-spoke wheels are held in place by four tabs originating from an inner hub is found on many Meier penny toys. This wheel arrangement was made in different sizes and proved to be very unstable. Although catalogue illustrations (probably taken from old blocks) show these wheels in the 1920s, in reality they were superceded around 1905. The hurdy gurdy player with his monkey is of Meier quality but this attribution cannot be conclusively confirmed.

409 B 52 mm

410 B 65 mm

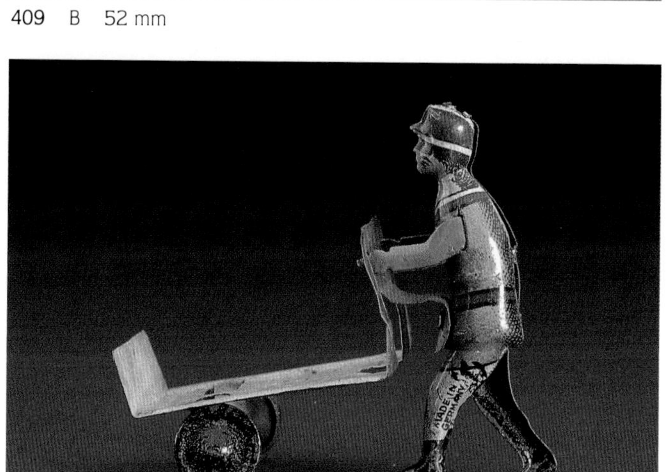

411 B 65 mm

412 D 80 mm

The porter, the black man in a rocking chair and the porter pushing the black man in his cart date from the 1920s and neither the tinplate used nor lithographic standards are of high quality. I believe these three toys to have been made by Georg Levy. The fourth toy of the man pushing a wheel barrow is common, but has not yet been conclusively attributed to any manufacturer.

413 C 105 mm

414 B 75 mm

415 C 75 mm

416 C 75 mm

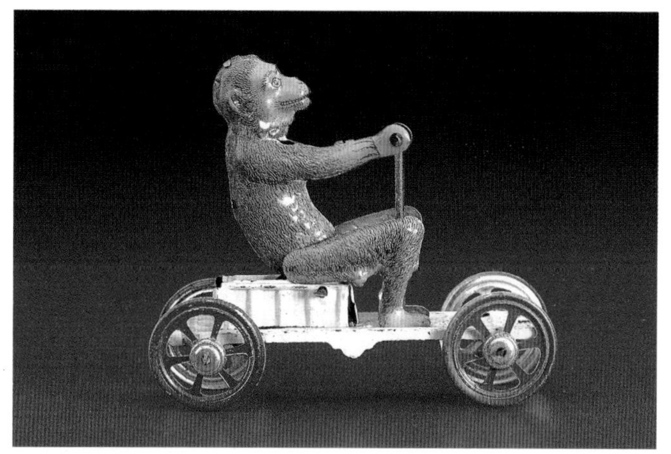

417 B 75 mm

413 This two-man flying Hollander was probably made by Kellermann in the 1920s.

414, 415 The rabbit and the boy feature high quality lithography and the wheels are typical of Georg Fischer. They are both almost certainly attributable to Fischer's pre-1914 production.

416, 417 These two flying Hollander toys were made by Meier. The example driven by the boy was certainly made both pre and post World War I.

418 The chinaman with the parasol is one of Distler's most elaborate and attractive penny toys from the 1920s.

418 D 80 mm

419 C 70 mm

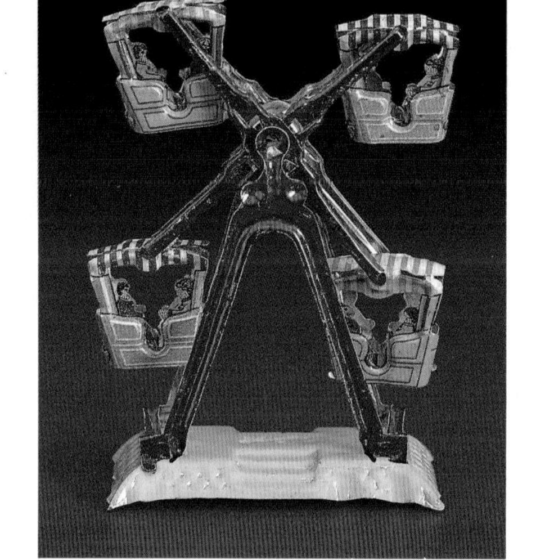

420 B 90 mm

421 C 70 mm

Detail of 419

Three Meier penny toys with a fairground theme. All date from the pre-1914 era.

423 B 77 mm

424 B 75 mm

Two Meier penny toys from the pre-1914 era. The six-spoke wheel with cast lead hub seen at the front of the walking rabbit is one of the designs that superceded the original four-spoke in about 1905 (see **407**). The rabbit with babies on her back was available in the 1920s and also came on a non-wheeled base.

425 C 97 mm

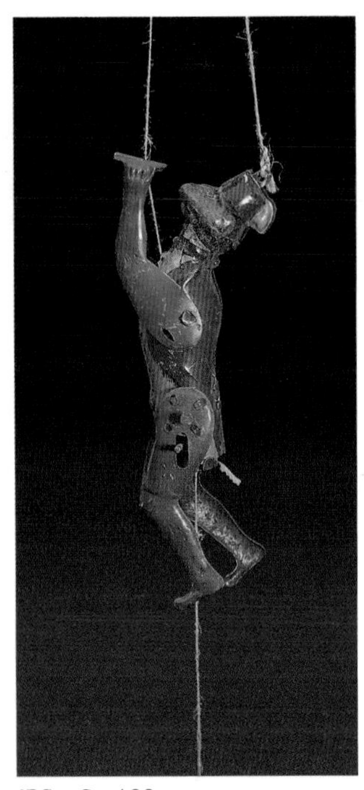
426 C 100 mm

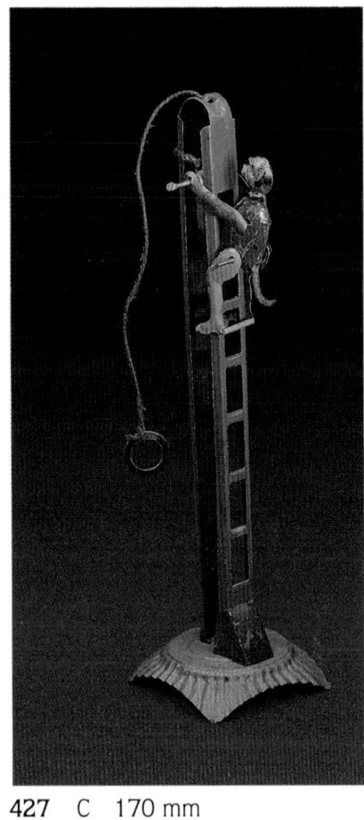
427 C 170 mm

428 D 215 mm

The two different versions of a climbing monkey are smaller and simplified versions of Lehmann's Tom No. 385. Their manufacturer has not yet been identified. The spiralling girls and the monkey which climbs a pole are from Distler's 1920s production.

429 C 240 mm high

430 B 120 mm high

431 B 120 mm high

The clown who somersaults on the bar as he rises up the pole was made by Distler in the 1920s. The handstanding clown is probably also by Distler. The parrot on a bar has a lead weight in the tail which aids in keeping him on his perch as he rocks back and forth. The manufacturer of this fine quality penny toy has not yet been identified.

432 C 75 mm

433 C 67 mm

434 B 85 mm

435 B 70 mm

436 C 100 mm

437 C 100 mm

438 C 100 mm

A group of penny toys with an equestrian theme. Several of the Meier examples had long production runs. **432** is by Fischer, **433** and **435–438** are by Meier, and **434** is by Kico.

439 A 65 mm

440 A 70 mm

441 A 80 mm

442 A 72 mm

There are many different rare early mechanical penny toys that are not attributable to Meier, although their themes were typical of that maker.

It is my belief that many of these exciting penny toys were made by Georg Fischer. Certainly the wheels used on the Great Dane with the monkey jockey and the horse trainer toys are typically Fischer. The identification of the maker of the two camel toys is less clear, but these could also be by Fischer.

(page 149)
443 Made by Meier, the production of this toy commenced around 1900 and continued for some 25 years. **445** is probably by Meier and is considered a much rarer toy.

443 C 100 mm

444 C 100 mm

445 B 95 mm

Detail of **443**

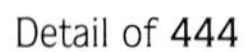

Detail of **444**

444 This is a copy of the Meier penny toy but originates from Italy. It was probably made in the 1920s or 1930s. The manufacturer has not yet been identified. Although basically similar there are many details omitted from the simpler copy. In particular note the lack of embossing on the cockerel's tail and the generally simplified pressing and lithography on the Italian toy.

446 C 75 mm

447 B 75 mm

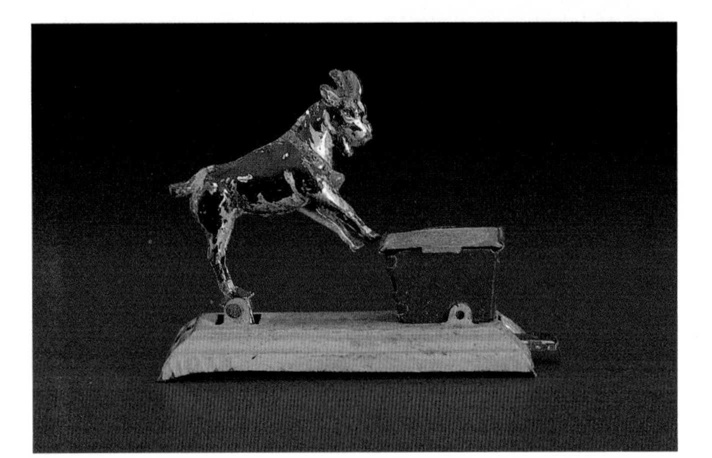

448 C 75 mm

449 C 116 mm

Four mechanical penny toys believed to have been made by Georg Fischer. When the chicken pecks at the egg, it opens to reveal a lithographed chick!

450 C 77 mm

451 C 60 mm

452 B 47 mm

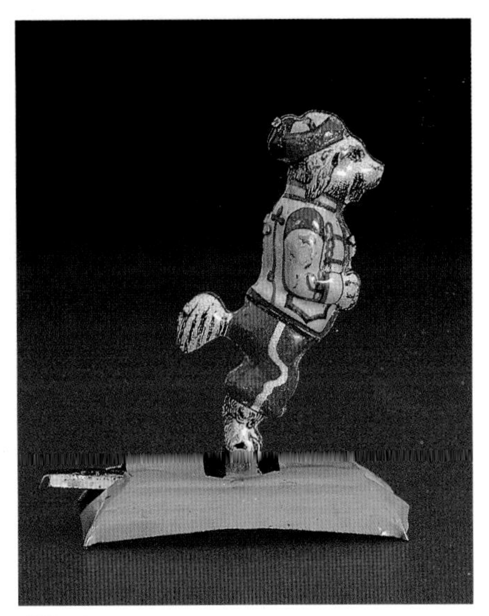

453 B 47 mm

The penny toy standing dog and standing rabbit are probably by G Fischer. The identity of the maker of the other two has not yet been established.

454 B 47 mm

455 B 47 mm

A group of six mechanical penny toys probably made by Georg Fischer based on combinations of a boy with a butterfly net, a toadstool, a frog and a butterfly. Together they form a most attractive set. At present there is no evidence that they were sold other than individually. It is interesting to note in the King Diary that the boy and butterfly in that collection was purchased on 24 December 1908.

456 B 100 mm

457 B 75 mm

458 B 100 mm

459 B 75 mm

460 B 75 mm

461 A 95 mm

462 B 47 mm

Six mechanical penny toys based on combinations of a boy, a pair of storks and a stork's nest. These are certainly by the same manufacturer as the previous set which I believe to be Georg Fischer.

463 A 95 mm

464 B 75 mm

465 C 47 mm

466 C 80 mm

467 C 90 mm high

468 D 90 mm high

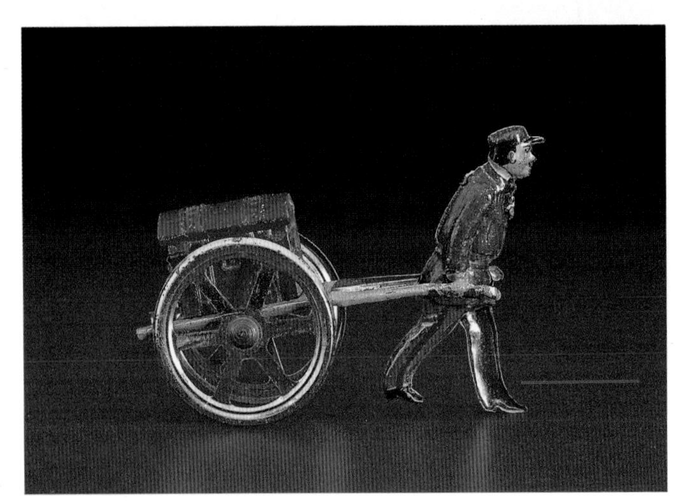

469 C 87 mm

466 An attractively lithographed porter pushing a trunk with a hinged lid. Possibly by Fischer.

467 Happy Joe has had the attentions of an imaginative restorer who, being dubious about successfully imitating the check trouser, fitted a tin wooden leg instead! This German toy bears the trademark B & U and K W.

468 The penny toy tap dancer similar to a miniature Lehmann 'Oh, My' is by Distler.

469 An early Meier toy in which the trunk has a sliding lid and could have been used as a candy container.

470 'My Word! If I catch you bending' is a mechanical penny toy that has flat figures. It is marked on the reverse side

470 B 100 mm

471 C 100 mm

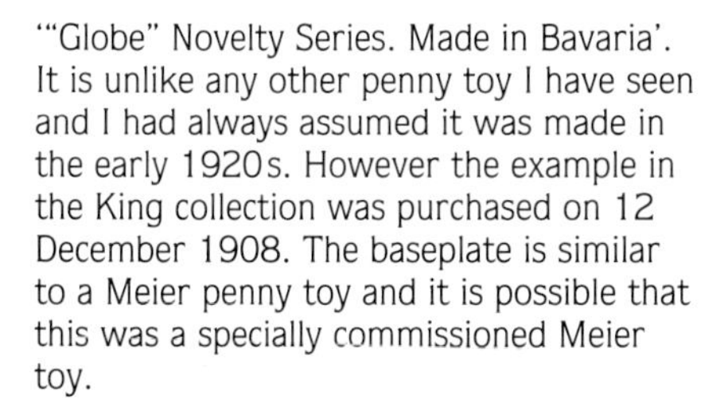

'"Globe" Novelty Series. Made in Bavaria'. It is unlike any other penny toy I have seen and I had always assumed it was made in the early 1920s. However the example in the King collection was purchased on 12 December 1908. The baseplate is similar to a Meier penny toy and it is possible that this was a specially commissioned Meier toy.

471 Mechanical dog in kennel, although unmarked, is made by the as yet unidentified company whose trademark is HMN (see page 345 of 1926 *The Universal Toy Catalogue*).

472 Believed to be by Meier, although the lever that activates the mechanical action is centrally placed rather than at one end. This is also found in the parrot and chicken penny toy (**445**).

472 A 95 mm

473 B 100 mm

The monkey soldier sitting on a dog rocker is by Meier. The ostrich trotting cart has all the hallmarks of Meier, while the identity of the bear and trainer is unknown. It is undoubtedly early and of good quality and thus might be by Georg Fischer.

474 B 75 mm

475 B 74 mm

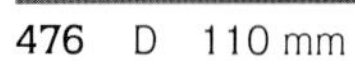

476 D 110 mm

477 C 100 mm

Several of the German tin toy manufacturers featured pool player toys in their production. Judging by the frequency with which they are found today, they must have been very successful sellers. One of the best known penny toys is Kellermann's pool player from the 1920s (**476**). The manufacturer of the other pool player (**477**) which is of heavier quality is not known.

478 This charming toy by Meier features a wheel under the nanny that has been stamped out to form five feet. As this rotates it effectively creates the impression of a rapid, short-paced walk. This toy had a long production run both before and after the First World War.

478 C 85 mm

479 C 90 mm high

480 C 90 mm high

Meier's very attractive Punch and Judy Show is found in several variations – the two illustrated and a simpler type with a much lower booth that was available in the 1920s. Stock & Co. is well known for its range of attractive clockwork vehicles and novelty toys. However they made one penny toy, a clown whose head and feet are weighted. There is also a Japanese copy of this toy.

481 C 70 mm

Detail of **480**

482 A whole series of pin-on mechanical penny badges were made in the 1920s. The action consisted of a moving part activated by pulling a cord. One of the most interesting is this toy of the Man in the Moon by an unknown maker.

483 Within the tin crown shape of this King Edward and Queen Alexandra Coronation souvenir is a paper strip depicting the coronation procession and ceremony that can be viewed through the lens. It dates from 1902 and is by an unknown maker.

484 When the crank handle is turned, a small tin plate moves behind the photograph to simulate a crude facial expression. An interesting 1920s penny toy of unknown make.

482 C 65 mm high

483 B 52 mm

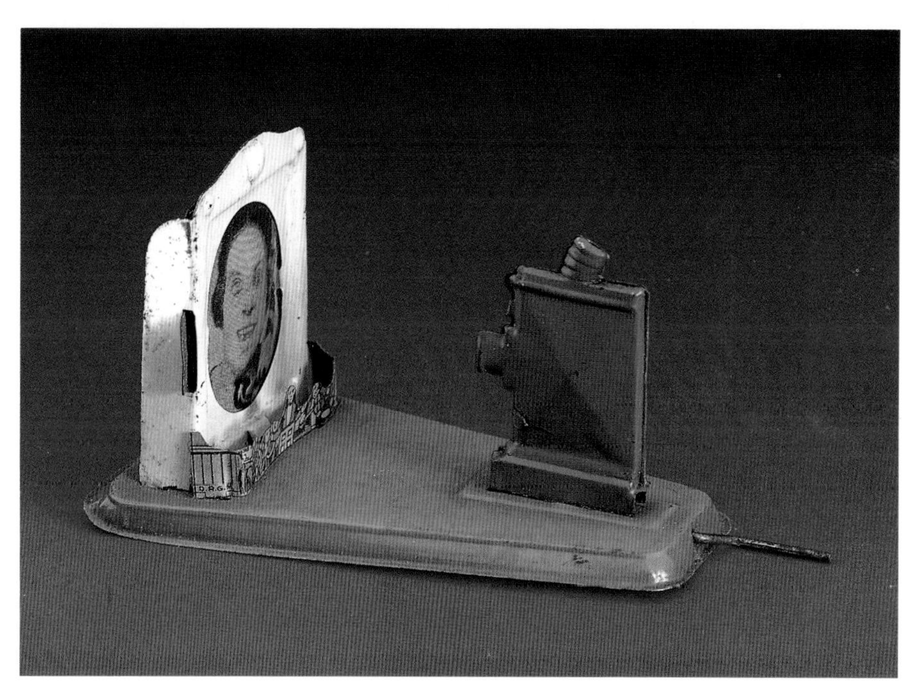

484 B 100 mm

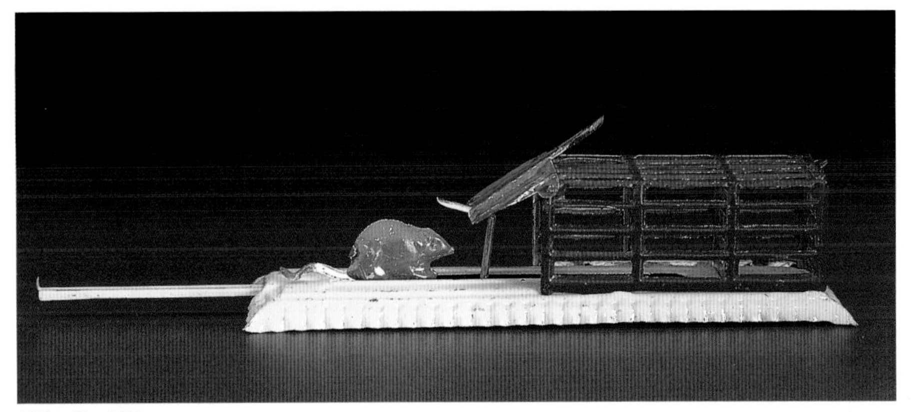

485 C 120 mm

486 74 mm

487 D 57 mm

488 B 60 mm

485, 487 The mousetrap and the two pecking geese are relatively common Meier toys. Both had long production runs. The mousetrap was also available with a shorter baseplate.

486 A marriage between two penny toys! The poodle comes from a Meier toy with a clown (see **395**). The wheeled base and the boy blowing a horn are by Fischer. I still do not know what should be at the other end of this penny toy. Both parts had lived for many years in my 'spares' box and one day I decided to experiment with the result as shown. Penny toys are extremely easy to modify and adapt and collectors must be careful not to purchase a marriage such as this one.

488 This is a small Japanese penny toy. Unlike many early Japanese toys, it owes nothing to European influence.

489, 491, 492 French penny toys are even less well documented than German ones. Generally they are spirit-painted tin, occasionally with some lead alloy parts as in the skipping girl whose body is a casting. All three of these toys were made by Henri Avoiron of Paris.

490 The double acrobat was made by Meier and was also available with a single figure.

489 B 82 mm

490 B 85 mm

491 B 82 mm

492 B 85 mm

493 A 65 mm

494 C 80 mm high

495 D 67 mm high

496 B 93 mm

497 A 75 mm

The boy scout and his dog (**493**) is one of Meier's earliest lithographed toys, c.1900. It is non-mechanical.

The double swing (**494**) by Meier was produced pre-1914 and post-1918. The single swing (**495**) is by Distler c.1920. The manufacturer of **496** is unknown.

The diabolo player (**497**) probably has the most complex mechanism of any penny toy; the action realistically simulates playing with a diabolo. Maker unknown.

AERONAUTICAL

498 C 100 mm high

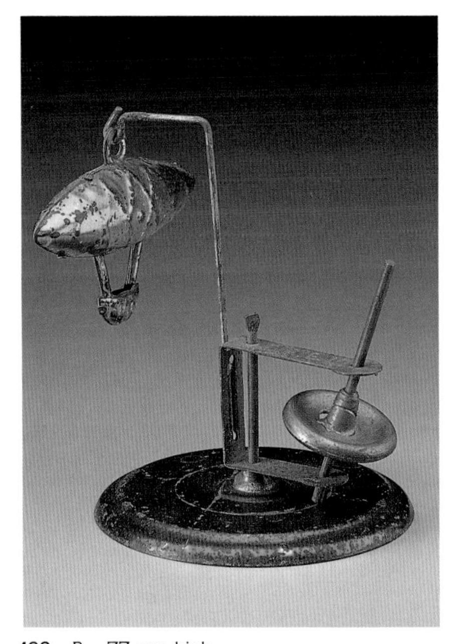

499 B 77 mm high

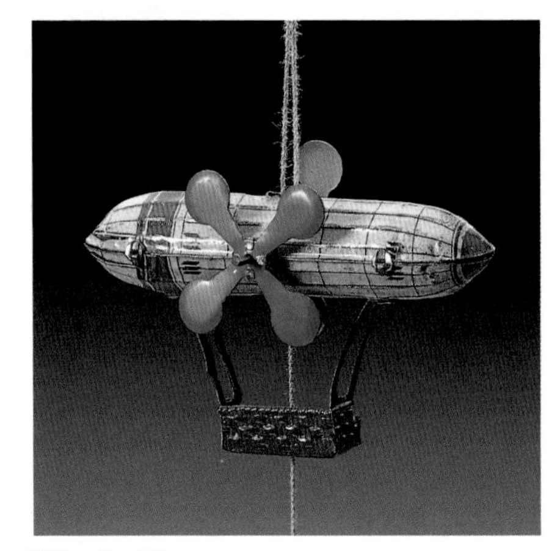

500 C 78 mm

498 A hot air balloon by Meier. A cord with a tin anchor at each end should run through the pulley.

499 An early spirit-painted dirigible, almost certainly German by an unknown maker.

500 The pulley mechanism and cord controls are identical to those found on Distler planes, so it is probably by this maker. However, it is marked 'ges.gesch.' which is commonly found on Meier penny toys and thus the attribution remains questionable.

Detail of **498**

501 C 78 mm

502 C 120 mm

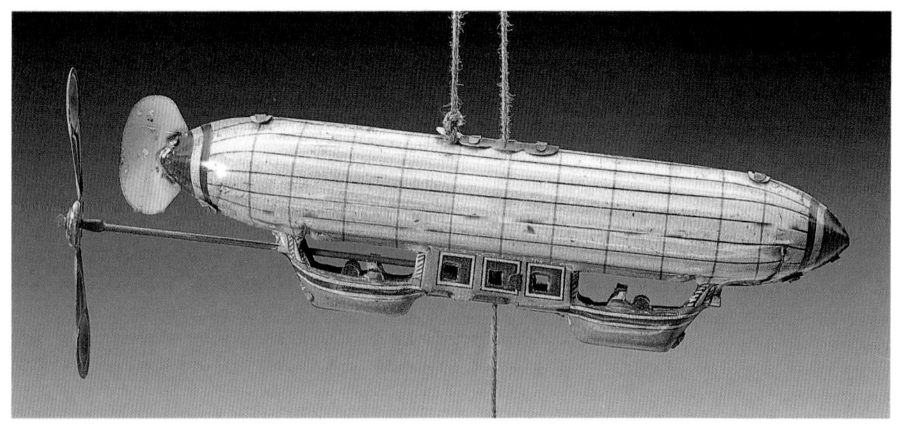

503 C 155 mm

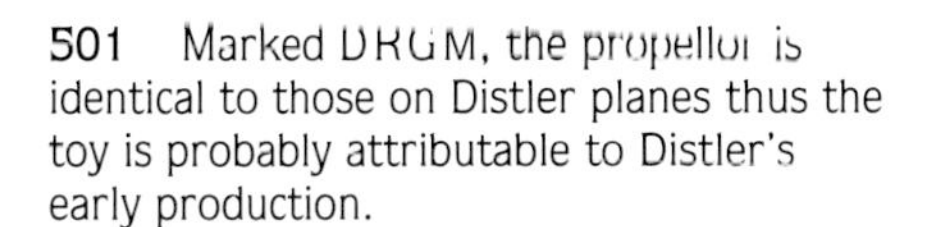

501 Marked DRGM, the propellor is identical to those on Distler planes thus the toy is probably attributable to Distler's early production.

502 A dirigible by Meier, which, when sold individually, had a cord with a tin anchor at each end running through it. The toy is commonly found on medium sized carousels marketed by Moses Kohnstam. Whether Meier made the carousels or supplied the penny toys to another manufacturer to fit onto their carousels is not known. Probably the latter theory is correct.

503 Probably by Distler, as the propeller and cord controls are identical to confirmed Distler products.

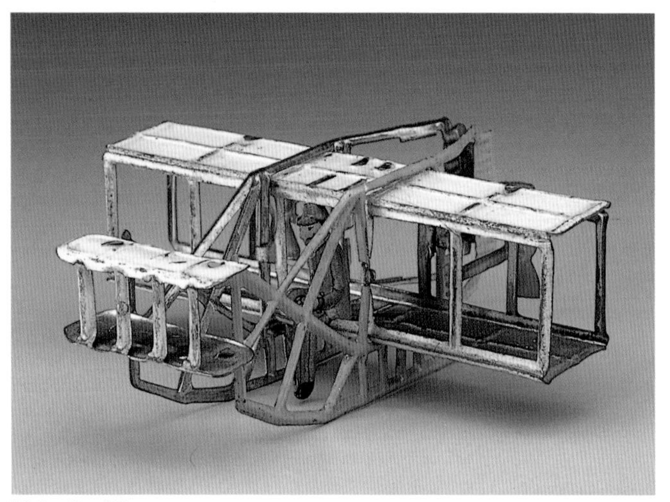

504 B 80 mm

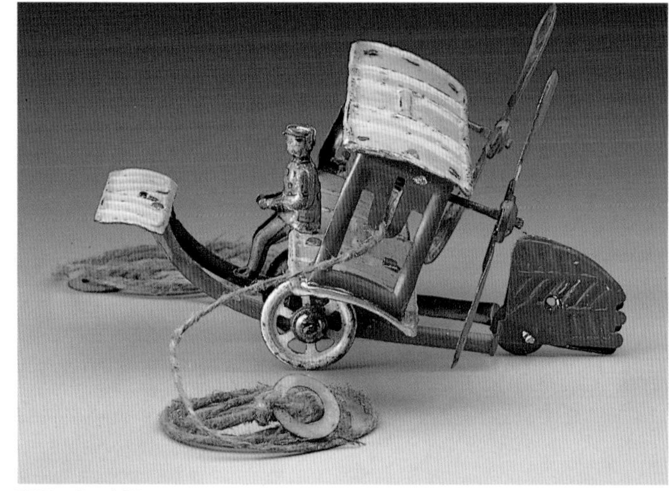

505 B 100 mm

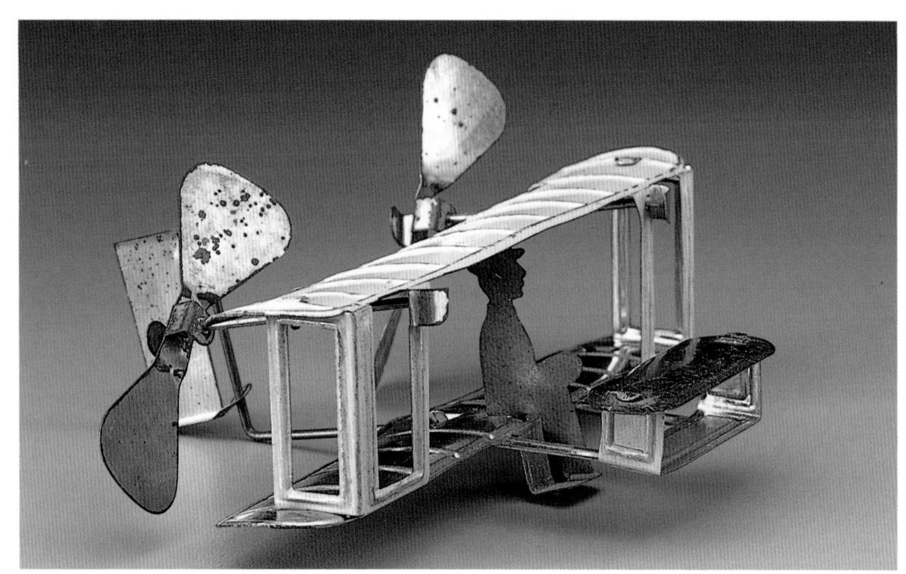

506 C 110 mm wingspan

504 This toy by Meier is the most attractive and desirable early penny toy plane.

505 Almost certainly a pre-1914 Distler product. The propellers rotate as the plane moves sideways across its cord.

506 An unidentified German penny toy plane that could be spun round a central pivot weight.

(page 169)
507 This toy bears the words 'Bleriot plane', 'Tip Top series' and 'Bavaria'. It features a Distler type propeller and string pulley, thus is probably by that maker.

508 This plane also features a Distler type propeller and string pulley, and may be reasonably attributed to that maker.

507 B 90 mm

508 C 83 mm

509 C 135 mm

510 C 185 mm

509, 510 Two classic Distler Bleriot type planes from the 1920s. There are many variations of this plane, including a version sold with a small tin lithographed hangar in which the pilot sits inside the plane rather than perched on the top. There is also a clockwork variant which performs a loop-the-loop manoeuvre around a central pylon.

511 E 140 mm high

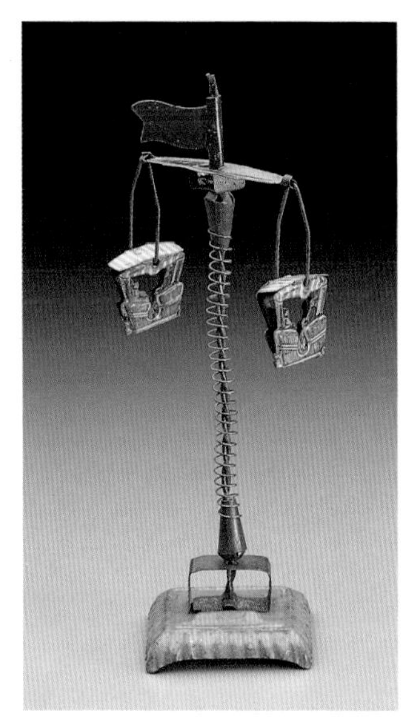

512 B 145 mm high

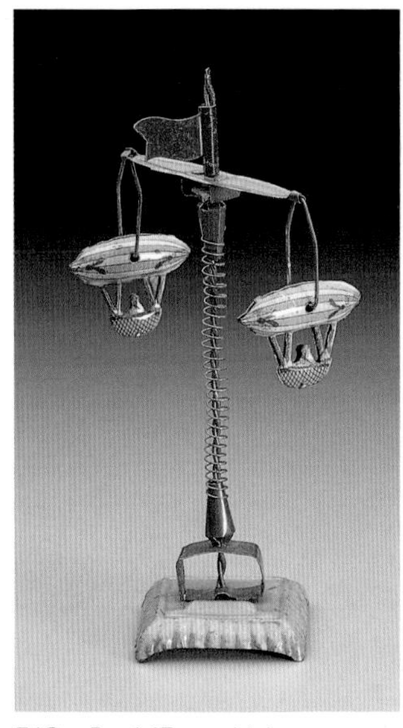

513 B 145 mm high

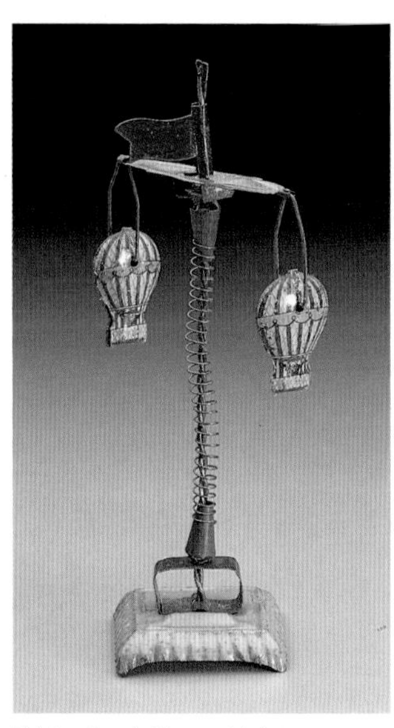

514 B 145 mm high

511 A 1930s toy of crude quality by Gebr Einfalt whose mechanism is activated by depressing and then releasing the spring. The two planes then spiral upwards.

512–514 These toys were probably made by Distler in the early 1920s. Available with the square tin base, or with a wire circular finger grip bottom. Almost certainly available in mixed combinations of balloon, dirigible and carousel gondola. Catalogue illustrations also show four units on one toy, i.e. two balloons and two dirigibles.

Detail of **514**

515 C 135 mm

516 D 130 mm

517 D 90 mm

518 D 130 mm

515 A typical Distler plane from the 1920s.

516–518 Three poor quality aeroplane toys from the 1920s which are probably by Kellermann.

OTHER MATERIALS

WHILST TINPLATE penny toys are the best known and recorded, it has already been noted that they consitute only a small percentage of total production. Almost any material of low cost, both natural and man-made, could be used to form a penny toy.

This section describes principally factory-produced examples, made from the most significant materials. Some of the home-produced penny toys which were made of natural materials such as bamboo, shells, nuts, bone, etc, are almost impossible to categorize and their existence is merely recorded.

A chromolithographic paper scrap c.1900

LEAD & CAST IRON

The casting of lead and tin into small decorative artefacts and Deity images goes far back into the antiquities of the Roman Empire. The abundance of these two malleable metals, mined in both Britain and Germany for centuries; their low melting temperatures and resistance to corrosion made them the commonest metals in everyday use through the Dark Ages and into Medieval and Tudor times. Lead was used for roof cladding, window frames and water containers, while pewter (75% lead, 25% tin) was almost the universal metal for utensils and drinking vessels.

The casting of small flat religious mementoes and saints' medallions became common throughout the Holy Roman Empire. These tokens were often confirmation of pilgrimage to the holy shrines and cathedrals of Europe. Despite their frailty, many of these pilgrim keepsakes survive today, such as rosary medallions, offertory gifts and saints' images, like those of St Thomas a' Becket of Canterbury.

These medallions were easily made, often by monks as a ready source of finance for the upkeep of their monastery or cathedral. The single-sided image was simply scratched to create a narrow gap between two flat pieces of slate or limestone, into which the molten lead was poured. After the Reformation in England and the spread of protestantism in Germany, the Low Countries and Scandinavia, the making of religious artefacts ceased except in France, Spain and Italy.

In Germany, these mould-making and casting skills were turned, in the early 1700s, to the production of domestic figures and, after the Seven Years War, the casting of tin soldiers. This cottage industry grew up around Nuremberg in Bavaria and to a lesser extent in Austria and France.

Johan Hilpert is probably the most famous and prolific of the early artists. His equestrian portrait of Frederick the Great, signed and dated 1777, plus the many Prussian regiments he produced, were the forerunners of an industry which employed thousands over the next 100 years.(27)

The Napoleonic Wars of 1800 to 1816 naturally gave great impetus and prestige to the flat tin soldier industry, so that engravers like Allgeyer, Raicke, Bunan and Schundler and Haffner in Furth prospered. In 1840, Ernst Heinrichsen started production of flats in Nuremberg and within thirty years eclipsed them all and was still active in the 1930s.

These millions of 'Zinnfiguren' were invariably sold collectively in split pine boxes, either by weight or number. It was only the large portrait figures and later ships and trains that were ever sold singly or in small dioramas.

LEAD FLATS

The lead flats grouped in plate **519** show a number of coaches and carriages of the 1860s. These could well have been sold individually and are typical of the earliest form of penny toy.

At the top of the photo are two quite significant flat castings, since they represent two of the first important transport milestones. The locomotive and carriage are inscribed 'Manchester and Liverpool' named after the first passenger carrying railway which opened on 15th September 1830. Were these sold as penny souvenirs on that historic occasion? Of some interest is the fact that the locomotive is not 'The Rocket' or 'Northumbrian' which opened the line on that day, but Stephenson's earlier 'Locomotion' of 1825, which ran on the Stockton and Darlington Railway. Likewise, the carriage is actually similar to the one pulled by 'Sans Pareil' during the Liverpool and Manchester Rainhill Trials of 1829. No doubt the artist who produced the mould only had engravings of these earlier locomotives and carriage to copy, as the Liverpool and Manchester Rolling Stock would not have been seen by the public until the inauguration day.

The paddle steamer with its tall funnel is obviously by the same maker and has been identified as the 'Victory' – the first regular cross-channel steampacket which started the Brighton to Le Havre route in 1829.(6)

The French staff car in the centre of plate **519** is dated about 1905–10 and is really at the end of the flats era. Whether it was sold singly or as part of a set with other vehicles or soldiers we cannot know. The small mounted Japanese semi-flat at the top right dates from the 1904–05 invasion of Manchuria and the defeat of the Russian Navy. Although it is a flat, it has a hollow horse made in a three-part mould.

The flat tin figures made in Germany for so long gave way reluctantly to the brief period of the semi-flat toy soldier. These were competing against the beautiful, but expensive, solid round lead soldiers of Lucotte of France, who, having merged with CBG-Mignot in 1875, were rivals to the German makers.

However, it was not long before Haffner in Furth started making high quality solid soldiers and, after the firm was joined by Heyde of Dresden, by 1890 the German industry once again dominated the markets of the USA, Britain and Europe. These soldiers were never sold singly and because of their high lead content were relatively expensive – toys for the rich.(27)

It was this lucrative world market that William Britain so rudely disrupted in 1893 with his patented hollow figures and horses. At one stroke, Britains more than halved the price of a box of soldiers. A one shilling box contained as many as ten infantry figures – each thus cost about a penny for the first time.

By 1905, Britains had become the largest manufacturer of lead soldiers in the world and was constantly challenging any copiers with copyright infringement writs. In addition, they sold very substantial numbers of gilt horses and infantry at 1d and 1/2d. These were seconds which were sold loose through village stores, market and fairground stalls, penny arcades and seaside toyshops.

At the same time as Britains were developing and patenting their hollow moulding process, using a lead alloy with 12% antimony, which has a lower melting point than pure lead, several small companies in Paris were perfecting highly detailed metal moulds which produced thin solid section lead alloy castings. These were the forbears of modern day gravity and pressure diecasting. Analysis has shown that these toys are made of an alloy of 55% lead, 42% antimony and 3% tin, which has unusual properties, similar to those which cause water to change to ice. These alloys expand slightly on solidification so filling the mould tightly to reproduce the finest detail, unlike the dense thick section lead of the solid soldier which actually shrinks away from the mould and does not carry any detail.

The new Parisian metal moulds were probably made of bronze and hand-engraved and were usually of three parts, comprising two outer blocks and a solid intersecting core. Over the years, the small models became more and more complex with moulds having as many as five loose, intersecting parts. These mould-making skills did not come from flat or even solid soldiers, but probably from silver smithing, ormolu and jewellery manufacture for which Paris was world famous.

The most prolific of these miniature toy makers marked their products with the initials SR, which for many years were known to toy soldier collectors as 'Rivollet', principally because they produced some of the cannons and limbers for the toy soldier firm of Mignot. Most toy soldier references do not mention Rivollet and even John Garratt's *The World Encyclopaedia of Metal Soldiers* dismisses Rivollet in a few lines and even dates the company to the 1950s.(14)

Research has indicated that this company must have been in production during the 1890s and was exporting substantially to Britain and America from 1910 through to the 1920s. They seem to have stopped toy production during the mid-1920s and possibly failed in the Depression of 1930–31.

The Rivollet premises at 3 Passage Perreur in Paris were

519 60–90 mm

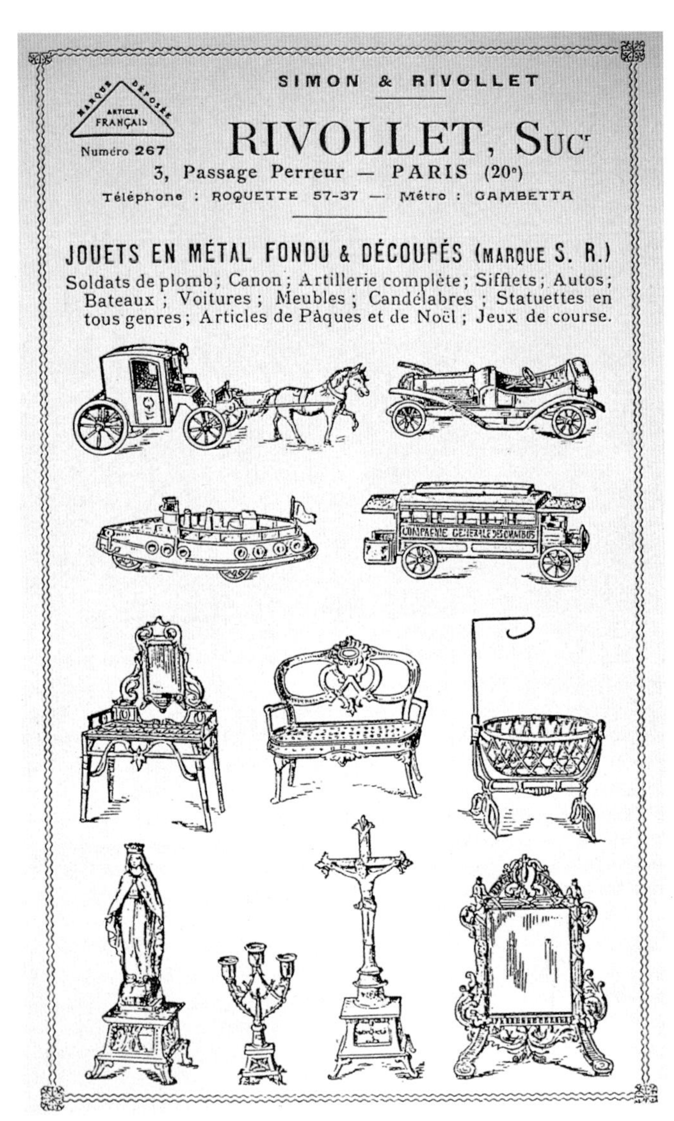
SIMON & RIVOLLET

RIVOLLET, Sucr

Numéro 267

3, Passage Perreur — PARIS (20e)

Téléphone : ROQUETTE 57-37 — Métro : GAMBETTA

JOUETS EN MÉTAL FONDU & DÉCOUPÉS (MARQUE S. R.)

Soldats de plomb; Canon; Artillerie complète; Sifflets; Autos; Bateaux; Voitures; Meubles; Candélabres; Statuettes en tous genres; Articles de Pâques et de Noël; Jeux de course.

520 Page from 1912 SR catalogue

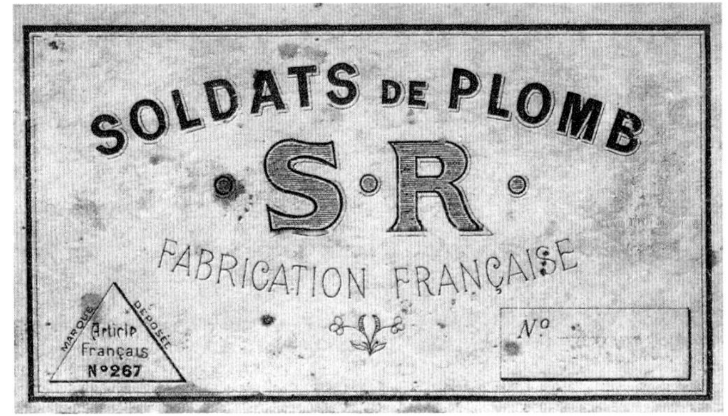

521 SR box lid label

substantial and could have accomodated more than 100 employees. In 1929, the company had moved to much smaller workshops around the corner but no further trace of their activities can be found in the 1930s. The author has identified over 200 different lead alloy penny toys by this quite prolific maker, many of which are shown in this book for the first time.

The company was first positively identified by a boxed set of soldiers and gun team (so many small toy makers can only be traced by this kind of good fortune). The box lid label is shown in plate **521** with a triangular trademark – 'Article Francais No 267'.

Research in the Register of Trademarks in Paris proved that this triangular mark was first granted in 1897 to 'Syndicate des Fabricants de Jouets et Jeux'. This was a trade cooperative of over 400 members, mostly in Paris, of toy and game makers. The Chambre Syndicate still exists to this day and some of their early archives have been preserved at the Musée des Arts Decoratifs in Paris, with whose kind permission the several pages of SR advertisements are reproduced – 1912 (**520**) and 1916 (**522, 523**).

126 LISTE DES MEMBRES ADHÉRENTS

ARTICLE FRANÇAIS

Numéro 267

SIMON & RIVOLLET

RIVOLLET Succr

3, passage Perreur. — PARIS (XXe)

TÉL. : Roquette 57-37 -- MÉTRO : Gambetta

JOUETS EN MÉTAL FONDU & DÉCOUPÉS (Marque S.R.)

Soldats de plomb; Canon; Artillerie complète; Sifflets; Autos; Bateaux; Voitures; Meubles; Candélabres; Statuettes en tous genres; Articles de Pâques et de Noël, pour la vente du 0 fr. 05, 0 fr. 10 et au-dessus, dorés ou décorés à la main.

522 Page from 1916 SR catalogue

LISTE DES MEMBRES ADHÉRENTS 127

ARTICLE

Numéro 270

SIMON & RIVOLLET

RIVOLLET Succr

3, passage Perreur. — PARIS (XXe)

Fonte à Façon dans tous métaux : aluminium, métal blanc, plomb, étain, etc.

Pièces détachées, petits robinets, roues, étriers, pour fabricants de Jouets en bois.

523 Page from 1916 SR catalogue

The SR company was originally started as a partnership of Simon et Rivollet, but some time around 1900, possibly after the demise of Simon, it changed its name to 'Rivollet Successors', so maintaining the original SR trademark.

The company produced such a wide range of cast lead alloy products, that several toolmakers must have been employed full time to keep up with the continuous output of new products in the 30 year period 1890 to 1920. They developed a distinctive style which enables many unmarked toys to be positively identified. Many are marked 'France', 'Déposé', or 'Made in France', both with and without SR.

After the First World War, the company brought out many memorial items such as Renault 'Char' tanks as inkstands, Art Deco photo frames and religious statues. No toys which would seem to date from the late 1920s have been found with the SR mark, although the same toolmaking techniques can be recognised in the products of AR (France), Johillco (UK) and Tootsie Toy (USA). All these three firms, so far apart, made very similar small lead cars, lorries and aeroplanes during the 1920s and early 1930s. Since it is highly unlikely that they copied each other, it is possible that there was a single skilled toolmaking source in Paris that supplied them all with moulds.

However, the production of Parisian penny toys cannot be solely attributed to the SR marque. Several have their own recognisable style and cryptic initials – LC; JC et Cie: V de V; CB & EF. To date, no further information has been found about these makers of very similar toys that can firmly identify their full names.(27)

These penny toys are found in virtually the same categories as their main competitors – the tinplate penny toys manufactured in Nuremberg described in the preceding chapters. These categories are (i) Horsedrawn vehicles from 1890 onwards (**524**); (ii) Motor vehicles from 1900 through to 1920 (**527**); (iii) Locomotive and carriages from 1890 (**528**); (iv) Ships from 1890 (**529**); (v) Aircraft from 1909 to 1918 (**530**); (vi) Cannons (**531**); (vii) Whistles (**532**); (viii) Dolls' house furniture (**534**); (ix) Miscellaneous items (**535**).

HORSEDRAWN VEHICLES

Horsedrawn vehicles were probably among the first products of the Rivollet company and its smaller Parisian rivals, but there is no nineteenth century information as yet to establish the starting date for these small lead alloy toys – the 1880s or early 1890s seem a possibility. The Syndicate triangular trademark was registered in 1897 and SR's numbers were 267 and 270, which do not help to establish a firm date, as the company clearly predates its official registration.

Plate **524** shows a selection of 26 horse drawn carriages, coaches and carts – both town and country styles – but some 45 distinct types by at least three makers have now been identified. They are all typically continental, including a goat trap and a dog milk cart. The latter is very common, invariably painted red with yellow wheels. There are two Ceremonial coaches. The one at top left is modelled on the Austrian State Coach, while the lower one bears a passing resemblance to the Lord Mayor of London's coach which is paraded once a year and was obviously a good occasion to vend to the crowds. There are two hansom cabs (by different makers), the lower bronze coloured one has 'The New Cab Co.' on the base. Was this an early promotional give-away similar to certain tinplate penny toys? There actually was a 'New Improved Cab Co' which operated 600 Hansom cabs in London between 1880 and 1907, when it changed its name to 'The London Improved Cab Co' with the introduction of the Marple Motor Taxi Cab.

The introduction of the motor car at the turn of the century meant that new models had to be introduced to be up to date, so what better than motorising an existing horsedrawn model? Plates **525** and **526** show how the

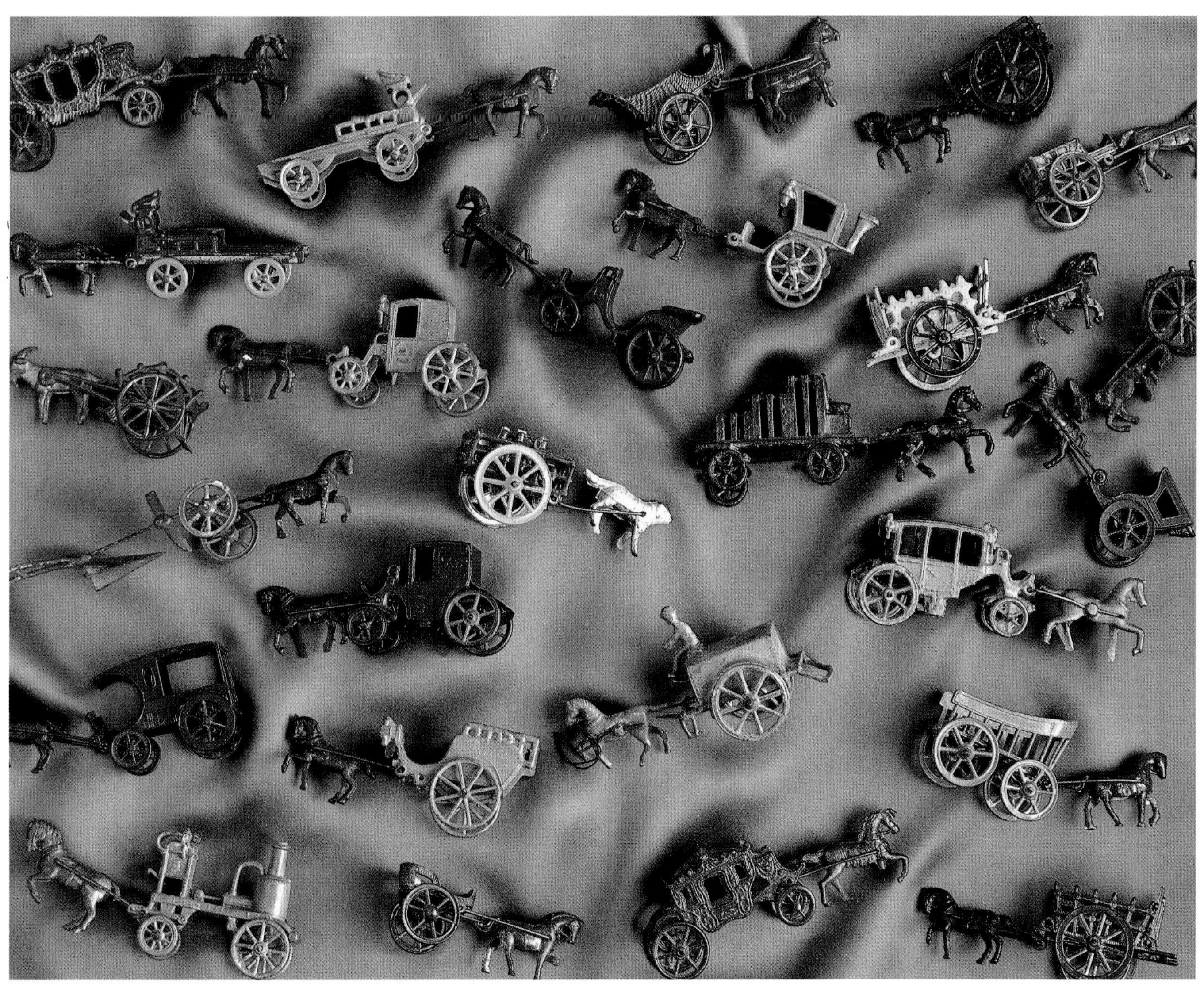

524 55–85 mm

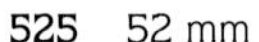

525 52 mm

526 coach 45 mm

coach mould has been altered by adding a bonnet and mudguards at the front, while the back half retains its original horse carriage springs. This type of change actually happened on real horseless carriages about 1903 or 1904, but the horse coach is still shown in the 1912 advertisement (**520**). Another interesting change, although quite minor, is the removal of the horse from the steam fire engine at the bottom left of plate **524** and the addition of the steering wheel to the same engine on the right of plate **527**.

MOTOR VEHICLES

Motor vehicles are easier to date than the horsedrawn ones, since we can assume that the toys are contemporary with the real vehicles. Plate **527** shows a selection of these quite accurate lead penny toys. The majority of SR models were bright copper-plated, which have darkened to bronze with time and handling. The use of grey paint usually dates the model to the 1914-18 war period. When a model has a red cross on it, it is clearly wartime issue, as can be seen in the 1916 advertisement in plate **523**. The racing car near the bottom left represents the 1903 Renault from the ill-fated Paris-Madrid Race in which Marcel Renault was killed. The other racing car, bottom right corner, has similarities with the 1912 Mercedes, although its rear is unusually bulbous.

The two buses must have been popular penny toys – if anything will sell on a street corner, a bus will. (Just as today the red London double-decker is still one of the best-selling souvenirs.) The General 'B' type bus was introduced in 1911. Two different SR versions are shown in plate **527**. They were either copper or grey (surprisingly never red) and must have been sold in large numbers, because they are quite common today, almost 80 years later. The Paris single-decker bus was also introduced in 1911. This model is so well-detailed that it can be positively identified as the De Dion Bouton 'DA', rather than the similar Schneider 'PB2' introduced in the same year.(5)

The red lorry and grey wagon with gun on the left are contemporary with the 1914–18 War. The latter is shown in the 1916 advertisement (**523**).

527 45–68 mm

528 40–70 mm

529 50–80 mm

LOCOMOTIVES AND CARRIAGES

Locomotives and carriages were an important part of the SR range and like the horsedrawn vehicles were probably made right through the company's life. It is obvious that they were sold in sets making up small trains and strictly speaking they are not penny toys, except as individual items. The small 0-6-0 locomotive (Nord No 1150) was based on a real pre-1890 engine while the larger PLM express is post-1912, the year the actual Pacific locomotive went into service.(17) These trains come in a variety of sizes as can be seen from plate **528**, and also many different colours in both passenger and goods versions.

Painting items light grey with red crosses in imitation of 1914–16 ambulance trains is an excellent example of toy-makers using topicality to sell toys. These now commemorate the return to Paris and other French cities of the horrendous casualities of the Somme in 1915. Such trains were popular toys. The small solo locomotives are especially common with many variations in casting and finish. However, it is not easy to find complete matching sets like those shown.

The small, somewhat cruder, four-wheeled locomotive and two wagons at the upper left is by an unknown maker, as is the long, grey, streamlined locomotive and carriages adorned with red crosses. This style of locomotive known as 'coupe-vent' was introduced on the PLM railway in 1898.

SHIPS

At first sight, the small, wheeled ships shown in plates **529** and **520** would appear to be figments of a fertile imagination, but in fact they are remarkably close to reality. France produced a number of high speed steam torpedo boats between 1887 and 1895 – fully ten years before Parson's 'Turbinia' proved to the British Admiralty in 1897 that a speed of 35 knots was not impossible. A contemporary postcard of 1892 shows that fact and fiction are the same.

530 Bleriot 60 mm wingspan, Taube 90 mm wingspan

The two battleships are also typical of the pre-Dreadnought ironclads of the 1890s.

At the top of the photograph is another interesting model. It bears the name 'Clermont' on its bow with the usual 'depose' and 'France' markings underneath. It so happens that 1904 was the centenary of the sailing on the Hudson River of this paddle steamer, the first steamship in America. (6) Was this little penny toy made especially for that faraway celebration? What is curious is that the identical model was announced in the 1921 Tootsie Toy catalogue for the first time.(41) Seventeen years after the centenary would seem to be a bit late. Our guess is that Dowst Bros bought the mould tools from Rivollet after 1920, along with other SR moulds.

AIRCRAFT

These early aircraft toys are probably the most important of the lead penny toys, because they so captured the public imagination.

The Bleriot toy seems to have sold in vast numbers all over Europe, and it seems that SR must have been producing the model quite soon after the channel crossing on 25th July 1909. This little model is quite accurately scaled and plate **530** shows a number of different versions, including one with 1914–15 French roundels. It is also shown in the 1916 advertisement (**523**).

Dowst Bros in America first started to sell the Bleriot models in 1910 (No 4482) some time before their first toy car was issued.(41) However, this aero model was made in a complex 4-part mould tool, requiring skills that did not exist in America at that time. Thus Dowst was probably just the importing agent for this best-selling model.

The SR Bleriot, clearly marked 'Made in France', is far and away the commonest pre-1915 diecast aeroplane, whereas the Dowst American version, which is unmarked, is extremely rare. Perhaps after 1920, Dowst bought the

531 40–75 mm

tools from SR as it was still shown in the 1925 Tootsie Toy catalogue (38) – not very enterprising given all the famous First World War fighters that were barnstorming America.

French model and soldier makers have always been most patriotic and nearly all SR models take their inspiration from French prototypes. Thus the small, grey biplane in the centre of plate **530** represents the Breguet 1, first flown at the Rheims Airshow in September 1909. On the left are two models, of which the bottom one is by SR and the one above is of unknown manufacture. They represent the 1914 Morane-Saulnier monoplane, the first successful allied fighter.(32) At the top left, the twin-engined aeroplane represents another Breguet, the 1918 bomber. Top right, can be seen a twin cockpit monoplane in which the wings are moulded as an integral part with the body. At first this model was unidentified, until it was discovered that the wings are on back to front and that the aircraft represents the 1910 Etrich-Rumpler 'Taube'.(32)

CANNONS

SR was a prodigious maker of cannons and plate **531** shows just a few of the many different styles and sizes (see also the 1916 advertisement plate **522**). The French '75' field gun in the bottom right hand corner was made in a large variety of sizes from the smallest 40 mm to an enormous 400 mm, almost in 40 mm steps. The siege cannon shown in the top of the advert was also made in similar sizes. These two guns were exported all over the world and can be identified in catalogues in France, England and America – Samaritaines (30), Gamages (1), Mace's (26), Montgomery (38).

The gun in the top right hand corner is intriguing because it is mounted in a stylized naval 4-wheel gun carriage (**522**). This gun was made in four sizes from the 50 mm penny toy shown to the largest at 120 mm. Much searching in military archives has not revealed whether

532 40–70 mm

there ever was an actual gun of this strange design. However, there is a very similar tinplate penny toy (see *Art of the Tin Toy* page 119 (33)) which lends credence to the existence of a real life model.

WHISTLES

The design of curious whistles to satisfy children's need to be noisy, appears to be a market niche that the Paris lead alloy casters cultivated more successfully than their tinplate or wooden toy counterparts, who produced very stereotyped penny whistles.

The selection shown in plate **532** has a representation of all the penny toy types – horsedrawn, cars, trains, ships, cannons, even the Bleriot aeroplane, but also unusual ones like the fish and key. A few are not immediately recognisable as whistles e.g. the horse cart, man with cannon and the 'Le Paris' ship.

The streamlined locomotive at top right, besides having wheels, contains a small cast fan to produce a siren-like noise, whilst the two guns at the bottom are early lead cap pistols (one of German manufacture). Close examination of several of these whistles – the fish, key and Bleriot, indicate exceptional moulding skill, because a fusible core (such as chalk, wax or salt) must have been inserted into the mould before casting, in order to produce the internal resonance chamber.

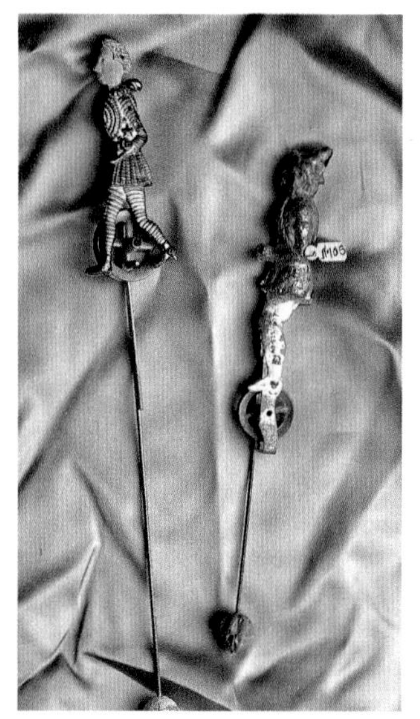
533 90–100 mm

534 55–75 mm

535 25–70 mm

536 55–60 mm

DOLLS' HOUSE FURNITURE

SR produced a very wide range of small lead alloy dolls' house furniture and household items. This market was obviously aimed at young girls of the Edwardian decade when furnishing a dolls' house was considered part of middle-class social upbringing. A small selection of these furnishings is shown in plate **534** and in the 1912 advertisement (**520**).

What is clearly evident is the extraordinary detail and embellishment that has been lavished on every piece by highly skilled craftsmen. Of special note are the folding high chair at the bottom and the very ornate folding push chair. Both of these chairs were produced by other manufacturers – Wm Britains in England and Tootsie Toy in the USA. The latter product is identical in every detail but only catalogued in 1925 compared to SR in 1912, thus we have to surmise that Dowst Bros acquired the mould tools.

MISCELLANEOUS

There are some SR toys which cannot be categorized. They produced so many novel and topical items of which plate

537 54 mm

538 coach 49 mm

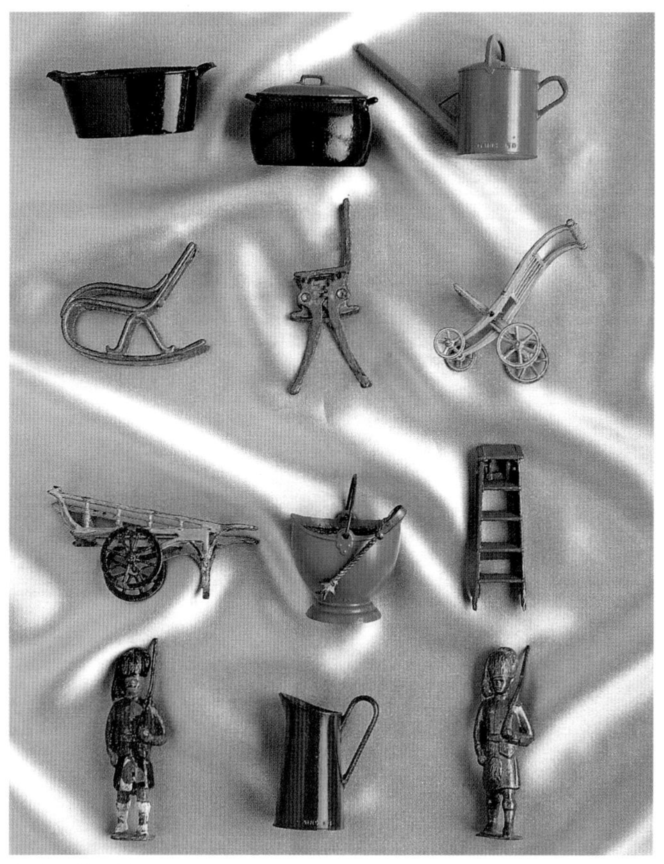

539 60–75 mm

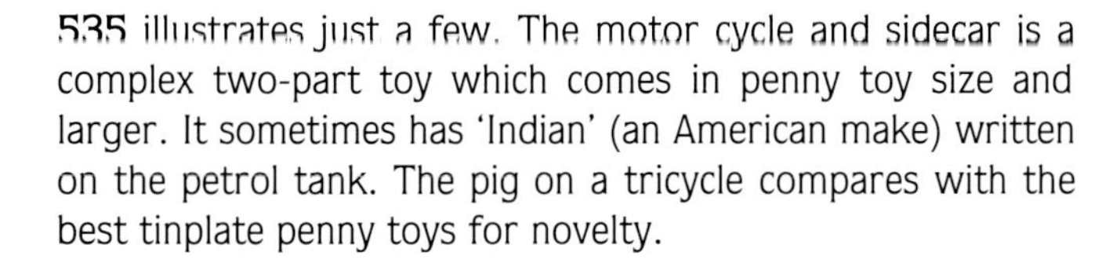

535 illustrates just a few. The motor cycle and sidecar is a complex two-part toy which comes in penny toy size and larger. It sometimes has 'Indian' (an American make) written on the petrol tank. The pig on a tricycle compares with the best tinplate penny toys for novelty.

It is interesting to make a direct comparison between a tinplate and a lead penny toy. The tightrope clowns in plate **533**, both bought in 1894 by Ernest King, are just such an example and illustrate the rival charms of detail versus colour.

The three delightful pieces in plate **536** demonstrate the

Cheap Toys and Novelties.

Intending Purchasers are respectfully requested to notice that the following Models and Designs being Copyright and Registered, they can only be obtained under the name W. BRITAIN, which should be specified when ordering.

Gilt Tea Pots and Coffee Pots. 1d. each. Registered Designs.
Miniature Kettles. In Gilt or Black Enamel. Registered Designs. Price 1d each.
Rocking Chairs. 1d. each.

Tea and Coffee Set in Hard Metal, Gilt. Price 6d. (Registered Designs.)

Miniature Saucepan. Finished in Black Enamel with bright Metal lid. Actual size. Price 1d. each.

Boiler in Copper, Gilt or Black Enamel. Price 1d.

Miniature Watering Pot, Finished in Red Enamel. Actual Size. Price 1d. each.

Gilt Kettle on Stand (Registered Designs). Actual Size. Price 2d. each.

Miniature Kitchen Set. Price 1/- Smaller size containing Saucepan, Kettle, Boiler, Teapot & Coal Vase, Price 6d.

Baby's Chair, 3 positions, High Chair, Low Chair, Rocker. 1d. each.

Push Cars. 1d. each.

Coster's Barrow in Blue or Gold. Price 1d.

Gilt Soldiers. (Copyright Models.)
No. 1—Horse ... Price 1d. each
,, 2—Horse ... ,, 2d. ,,
,, 3—Foot ... ,, 1d. ,,
,, 4—Foot ... ,, $\frac{1}{2}$d. ,,
,, 5—Horse ... ,, $\frac{1}{2}$d. ,,

Coal Vase (in Copper, Gilt or Black Enamel). Price 1d.

Steps. Price 1d.

Beautifully Designed Model of the Football Association Cup. Registered Design. Silver or Gilt. Actual Size. Price 1d. each.

Zulus, Assorted Colours ... ... 1d. line
Crawling North American Indians, Asstd. Colours ..
Large Painted Highlander ... ...

MISCELLANEOUS CASTINGS.

Jockeys, Bicycles, Warships, Yachts, etc., in several qualities and sizes for Race Games, &c. Prices for same on application.

540 Page from 1910 Britains' catalogue

extraordinary modelling skills which can capture such fluidity of movement and detail in these tiny toys. The fineness of the casting of the equestrienne, the clowns and the fighting soldiers has surely never been bettered. These examples are from the King collection, now in the London Museum, which were bought between 1893 and 1918. Just over nine per-cent of the 1703 toys in the King collection are diecast items.

The Christmas tree ball at the top centre of plate **535** is another remarkable casting. It appears to have no joints or seams. As with the whistles previously described, one has to assume that a fusible ball of plaster or wax must have been loaded into the hemispherical tool halves before casting. This would then be removed by washing or melting after solidificaiton of the metal to produce the hollow centre.

The two close-ups of vehicles shown full size in plates **537** and **538** illustrate the intricate embellishments of flowers and garlands that the Parisian artisans added to even the simplest toy. The heraldic shield on the ceremonial coach despite being only 4 mm across has still been quartered – such detail beyond the call of duty shows the toy maker taking pride in displaying his skills.

Although SR and the other Parisian casters created a niche market for these lead alloy penny toys, it was relatively small when compared to the millions of tinplate penny toys that poured out of Germany, especially from J Ph Meier, Georg Fischer and others covered in earlier chapters. They also had stiff competition from the pewterers of Germany with their worldwide sales outlets, especially in dolls' house and dolls' size utensils and artefacts.

Even William Britains obviously thought there was a worthwhile penny toy market – their 1910 catalogue contains a whole page of 'cheap toys and novelties' at 1d each (**540**)(7). A selection of these very 'domestic' penny toys, which are no doubt intended for young female customers, are shown in plate **539**. Britains considered attractive bright

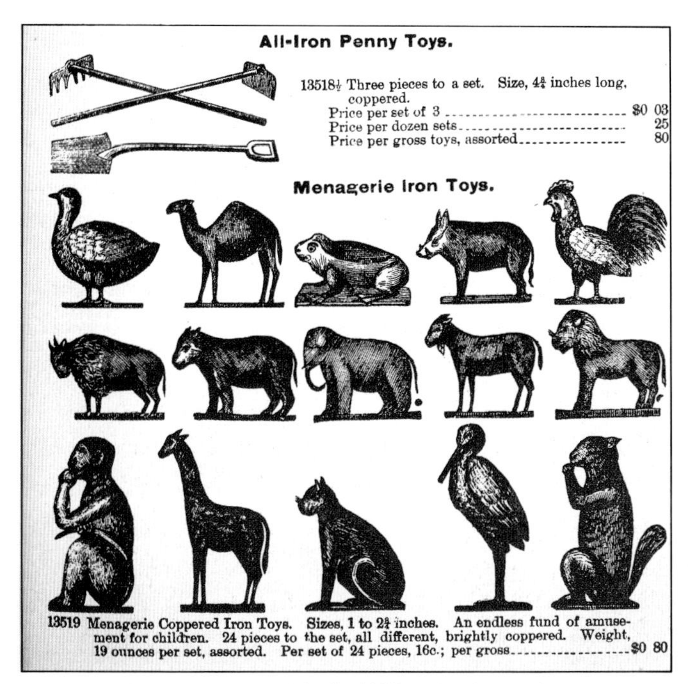

All-Iron Penny Toys.

13518½ Three pieces to a set. Size, 4¾ inches long, coppered.
Price per set of 3 .... $0 03
Price per dozen sets 25
Price per gross toys, assorted 80

Menagerie Iron Toys.

13519 Menagerie Coppered Iron Toys. Sizes, 1 to 2¼ inches. An endless fund of amusement for children. 24 pieces to the set, all different, brightly coppered. Weight, 19 ounces per set, assorted. Per set of 24 pieces, 16c.; per gross $0 80

541 Page from Montgomery Ward's 1896 mail order catalogue

colours important, whereas SR used copper plate or grey paint. At the bottom of the plate are examples of a gilt soldier and a large painted highlander.

A comparison between Britains' folding high chair and folding push chair and the similar items by SR (**534**) show most graphically the difference between the stark almost utilitarian simplicity of the London maker and the ebullient Rococo style of the Parisian craftsmen of Rivollet. However, Britains did have a small Paris factory between 1905 and 1915, so we must wonder if they were influenced by Parisian casting techniques (20).

CAST IRON

The American toy market between the 1880s and 1905 was dominated by the indigenous cast iron and iron sheet toy manufacturers. Every mail order and stores catalogue had pages and pages of cast iron fire engines, horsedrawn vehicles, circus, bell toys, mechanical and still banks and those ugly hill climbers. These items were particularly American and there was no equivalent in Europe with the exception of Wallwork of Manchester, England, who made several cast iron floor trains.

However, in the 1890s, German and to a lesser extent French tin toys came onto the American market. By 1900, the German imports to America were having a serious effect, taking a greater and greater share of a rapidly expanding market. As far as penny toys were concerned, the German tinplate toys were supreme. As can be seen in the preceding section, even special promotional penny toys were commissioned from Germany because there were no equivalent cheap and attractive toys made in the USA. Many of the later 'Crackerjack' toys given with that famous brand of popcorn were imported. An entry in Montgomery Ward's mail order catalogue of 1896 shows a range of 'All-Iron Penny Toys' (**541**)(38). These are simple sets of miniature garden tools and a menagerie of 1" to 2½" animals. As can be clearly seen there is no attempt at animation – no pull-along wheels, no moving legs or heads.

These uninspiring penny toys did not last long as no other catalogue entires can be traced. Meanwhile, LH Mace in their 1907 catalogue still carried a list of 'Coppered Penny Iron Toys' – hatchets, hoes, rakes, lawnmowers and shovels, etc – all at $0.75 per ½ gross wholesale!(26)

The dollar to the pound sterling was rock steady from 1900 to 1920 at an exchange rate of 4.8 dollars to £1. This is 2 cents to 1 penny so that these iron 'penny' toys were almost exactly 1 cent each to retail at 2 cents.(24)

CELLULOID

CELLULOID, or to give it its proper chemical name, cellulose nitrate, first went into production in 1870 and was the first commercially produced plastic material. It was produced from cotton fibre waste by the action of nitric and sulphuric acid. Various grades were made varying from lacquers to film (early silent cine film), sheet and rod.

The original Victorian uses for this new easily moulded material were for imitation horn, tortoiseshell and translucent marble and pearlite. These were especially useful for hairbrushes, combs, toothbrushes, soap trays, knife handles and many household articles. It was also used in early fountain pens, spectacles frames, women's high heels and piano keys imitating ivory. The first trade name under which the material was marketed was Zylonite and it was known by this name in the USA, while Xylonite became the usual name in England. (British Xylonite Ltd – BXL) (39)

It wasn't long before toymakers were using this material, especially the doll makers who found a very cheap alternative to bisque or papier mâché for heads, limbs and bodies. Thin sheet celluloid is very easily moulded into complex hollow shapes, by pressing, inflation, or vacuum forming, and as a consequence created a whole new regime of cheap toys.

It was the Japanese who really developed the use of celluloid for toy production from the 1920s right through to the 1950s. They were undoubtedly the largest manufacturers in the world, often successfully combining it with tinplate and clockwork motors.

It is known that some production of celluloid toys, other than dolls, was undertaken in Germany before 1910 with items such as clockwork fish and divers. Lots of floating ducks, swans and frogs for bathtime play were made of this very waterproof material.

When this book was planned, it was not known that celluloid or zylonite penny toys existed in any quantity or quality. Quite by chance a collection of 80 quite unique celluloid penny toys has recently been discovered. They had been preserved by a seventy-year-old lady since they were given to her in 1927 by her grandfather.

The story of their origin is touching and illustrates the often strange and sentimental reasons why toys come to be saved for future generations. The toys were bought on a regular basis for a small invalid boy (born 1907 – died 1920) by his father before and during the First World War. On trips into the Essex countryside between 1910 and 1915, they were bought from a village shop in Great Bentley and hidden in games of hide and seek for the little boy to find.

These interesting toys do not seem to have any parallel with any other penny toys made of wood, tinplate or cast metal. None of the 60 or so toys shown in the following plates has any maker's identification mark, but a few have DGR or Germany embossed on the celluloid, which was necessary for export purposes. Luckily the 1914 mail order catalogue of Butler Bros shows a few of these 'Zylonite Toy Novelties', called 'Rolly Polies' (**542**).(38)

The toys have been grouped in their various types:

SPHERICAL LEAD BASE

Plate **543** shows a collection of character figures. On the left are Bismark, Father Christmas, a Chinaman with pigtail, and other folk figures; on the right, three German officers with pickelhaube hats. A group of children and animals are illustrated in plate **544**. These small toys have much the same sort of humour as Snoopy and Peanuts today. There are Easter chickens at the left. The green-jacketed boy with the pull-out tongue is grotesque – could he be Buster Brown? In plate **545** can be seen a host of smaller Rolly Polies, which can be compared with the advertisement in plate **542**. The fat gentleman with glasses, bow tie and waistcoat can be seen in all the types of celluloid toy (see **543**, **548**, **549**). Is he 'Foxey Grandpa' – an American comic character, 1903–04?(25)

ZYLONITE TOY NOVELTIES

ZYLONITE ROLLY-POLIES.

Weighted bottoms, always right themselves.

F3140—2¼ to 2½ in., 16 styles, figures with painted costumes, cats and dogs in natural colors. Asstd. 2 doz. in box............... Doz. **40c**

Two styles F3142

F3142—2¾ in., 12 styles, up to date characters, painted features and costumes. Asstd. 1 doz. box. Doz. **72c**

Two styles F3143

F3143—3⅛ in., 6 styles, chubby boys and girls with tinted costumes, natural color cats and dogs, painted features. Asstd. 1 doz. box. Doz. **95c**

Two styles F3144

FLOATING ZYLONITE FIGURES.

4 styles, asstd., swan, frog, fish and duck, natural colors, float in lifelike manner, for baby's bath, acquariums, etc.

F3148—About 3⅛ in. 2 doz. in box. Doz. **33c**

F3149—About 4⅛ in. 1 doz. in box. Doz. **80c**

RUNNING ZYLONITE MOUSE.

F3132—2⅝ in., natural color body, painted features, spiral wire tail, heavy metal roller on pivot, when pushed runs in lifelike manner. 1 doz. in box................Doz. **45c**

ZYLONITE BALANCING BIRDS.

Note—By cutting beak card can be inserted, excellent favor or price ticket holder.

542 Page from Butler Bros mail order catalogue

543 45–55 mm

544 35–50 mm

545 45–50 mm

WHEELED

These wheeled character figures feature 20 mm wheels from tinplate penny toys. Plate **546** illustrates, at left, a Red Indian Chief, Kaiser Wilhelm, Uncle Sam, female figures associated with the Munich Beer Festival carrying a steiner and hops. The figure in the centre has tiny hands on springs, while at right are a policeman, Father Christmas, Bismark and a hippopotamus. In Plate **547** can be seen a close-up of a wheeled Bismark in sailing hat with excellent facial features.

LEAD ROLLER BALL

Plate **548** shows a group of lead roller ball character figures. This was another interesting method of introducing movement. The beer and hops female is a traditional harvest symbol. The small cars on the right have lead rollers.

SPRING-MOUNTED

In plate **549** can be seen a group of spring-mounted character figures. On the left, Louis Wain cats (compare with the advertisement in plate **542**), Santa Claus, a West Point cadet, the American President Woodrow Wilson, et al.

These penny toys have surprisingly political overtones in the way they lampoon well-known individuals. Historians will no doubt be able to put more names to some of these miniature 'spitting images' from the early 1900s which have a unusually American slant. Remember, however, that the USA was Germany's largest toy market and popular comic characters have always been best-sellers, just as the Walt Disney characters are today.

547 38 mm high

548 45–50 mm high

546 38 mm high

549 75 mm high

WOOD

THE CARVING and painting of wood in the forested, mountainous regions of Germany, Austria, Hungary and Switzerland have been carried out for many centuries. In all these areas, it was the turning of domestic furniture and utensils that was a traditional craft. In time, the carving of other objects gradually increased to become a skilled craft that could earn a living. In Germany, by the sixteenth century, wood carvers in Nuremberg and Sonneberg were organized in Town Guilds.

The production of the first primitive toys such as balls, skittles and dolls' heads started in the late sixteenth century. These items, which were painted with bright bismuth lacquers, were made in remote mountain valleys over the winter months in villages like Oberammergau and Berchtesgaden in Bavaria. These toys were collected in spring by agents and taken to Nuremberg for sale at the important annual toy fairs.

Other areas which became important producers of wooden toys by the seventeenth century were around Sonneberg in the Thuringian forest 100 kilometres north of Nuremberg and the Groden Valley in the Austrian Tyrol (Italian since 1920).

In 1733, thousands of skilled turners and carvers of Berchtesgaden and Saltzburg, across the border in Austria, migrated north to Sonneberg when the 'Peace of Westphalia' guaranteed protestants freedom from persecution. Thus Sonneberg became an important toy centre by 1800, while in southern Bavaria cottage industry declined.(13)

However, it is the Erzgebirge region south-west of Dresden in Saxony that became the major wooden toy producing area of Germany. The region's prosperity originally relied on the mining of lead, tin and copper which collapsed at the beginning of the nineteenth century, with the competition of tin from Cornwall and the exploitation of the Falun copper mountain in Sweden. Some of these miners organised the first wood turning factories.

By the 1850s, Erzgebirge wooden toys were world famous, especially for Noah's Arks, animals, soldiers and dolls. Like the tin soldiers made around Furth and Nuremberg, the Erzgebirge and Sonneberg small wooden toys were sold in collective groups attractively displayed in boxes and put together to bring added value and sales appeal to what were essentially quite cheap toys. (13) Many seemingly individual pieces in collections today were once part of large sets.

Wooden toys had the market much to themselves in the 1850s and 1860s, but by 1900 the lithographed tinplate toy had taken the major share of that toy market away – such is progress. Wood was not really suitable to produce the detailed realism needed in ships, trains and that newfangled invention, the motor car. But in penny toys, wood could compete and thus a large number of small horsedrawn vehicles, trams and cars appeared around the 1900s. These little toys are still being made today, but the numbers declined in the early 1930s when diecast toys became so popular.

The 1924 *Universal Toy Catalogue* (40) shows many of these wooden penny toys (virtually unchanged from before the First World War) in selection boxes of 50. It is clear that the retailer would sell individual toys at 1d, 2d or more for the larger items. (**550**)

Just a sample of small Erzgebirge penny toys spanning the years 1900 to 1930 are shown in plate **552** and include early horsedrawns, trams, motor vehicles, a train and even a 1914–18 aeroplane. In amongst these are some carved articulated figures of sailors which are much older. These well-painted little figures are probably from the 1890s and represent a whole genre of carved miniature figures that appealed to Victorian children.

Even earlier are the six bristle toys in plate **551**. Their quality and attention to costume detail is remarkable for objects so small (45 mm). It is said that they were bought by Victorian ladies who put them on their pianos, to dance

550 Page from the 1924 *Universal Toy Catalogue*

when they played.(8) They are made from wood, paper, moulded plaster and four bristles to hold their swinging legs free. In *The Illustrated History of Toys* it is mentioned that they were made in the Thuringia area (i.e. Sonneberg) in the middle of the nineteenth century.(13) To the author the costume appears to be from further east, either Bohemia or Moravia (now Czechoslovakia), which has been confirmed by the Goethe Institute.

MATCHBOX

Another fascinating style of penny toy, which was made from the turn of the century to well into the 1930s, was a great favourite with children. These were the little toys that were fitted into ordinary matchboxes. They are a typical Erzgebirge product which being so fragile unfortunately do not survive very often. London street vendors are often depicted as disabled war veterans selling matches and boot-laces. Perhaps they were really selling matchbox penny toys, bringing pleasure to thousands of children.

There are five main types of matchbox penny toys as shown in plate **553**:

1 The 'smallest' – kitchen, train, schoolroom, workshop, sickroom – small tableaux with furniture and tiny figures.

2 Miniature games – draughts, chequers, lotto, solitaire.

3 Construction toys – battleship, aeroplane, ark, sleigh, carriage.

4 Trick and joke toys – pop-up mice, conjuring tricks, jumping frogs and wooden puzzles.

5 Small products – musical instruments, tiny dolls (both wood and celluloid), furniture, bottles etc.

These rare little toys were nearly all made in Germany, but from the late 1920s, they were also produced in Japan and India and imported into the UK. 'Fairylite' is the trademark of one such Japanese toy importer in London.

551 45 mm high

552 40–80 mm

The SLEIGH
in the match-box
National-Art-of
Sick-Room
Match-Box
The smallest School in the world
Die kleinste Schule der Welt
D.R.G.M.
LOTTO
National-Art-of
Hoop-turning & Wood-carving
Match-Box
The carriage
Erzgebirgische Volkskunst
Zündholz-Schachtel
FATHER'S FAILING
Allgäuer
Bauernstube
D.R.G.M.
D.R.G.M.
battle ship in
match-box
Miniature-chequer
MADE IN GERMANY
Fairylite
SAFETY MATCHES
IMPREGNATED
The smallest
Kitchen
D.R.G.M.
The AEROPLANE
in the match-box

553 50 x 35 mm

GAMES

Many different kinds of small, cheap wooden games were produced to amuse children on train journeys, for Christmas stocking fillers, or for party prizes. Plate **554** shows two typical examples – a table croquet set and skittles, but there were also small jigsaws, bagatelles, hooplas and of course, tops. The Filippino Solitaire is an American 5 cent toy (**555**) with a leaflet stating "even the baby wants one".

Whilst new production methods could increase the output of tinplate toys to keep pace with the rapid inflation in the early 1920s – actually dropping in price – the traditional methods used for wooden toys were slow and much more expensive.

Besides, the young customers were more sophisticated and wanted mechanical moving toys and talking dolls. Therefore at the bottom end of the market there were totally new influences in operation, which, when combined with the parental revulsion against war toys, brought other products to the fore. One such line was Britains' 'Home Farm Series' of lead animals, farmers and vehicles. Although these toys were sold in attractive boxed sets, Britains made a deliberate policy to sell any and all as individual items. Thus children could spend from their pocket money, a 1d on a cow, horse or figure, 1/2d on a ship or pig and even less for the chickens and lambs. The animals and people were so realistic that it is not surprising that the stereotyped Erzgebirge figures and animals were rejected.(21)

We can see a definite lowering of standards on wooden penny toys during the 1920s in order to hold prices. Plate **556** shows how far the 1d toy had deteriorated by this time. Six boxes of unsold 1920s penny toys were found in the cellar of a Scottish toyshop, complete with 1d paper bags.

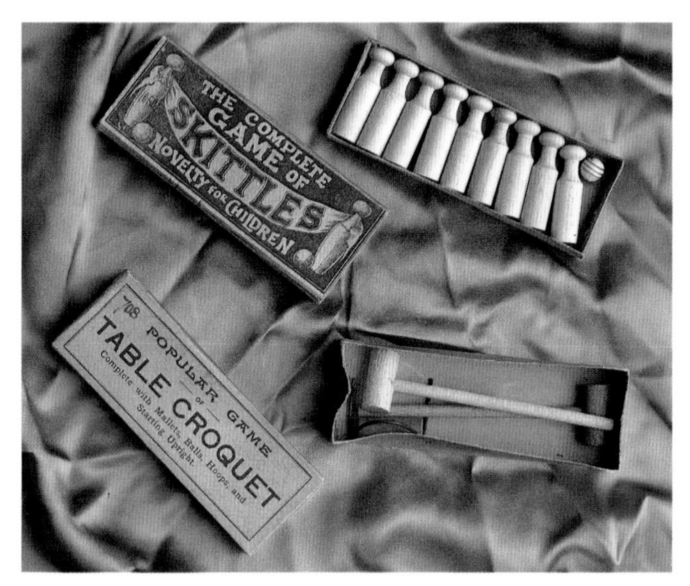

554

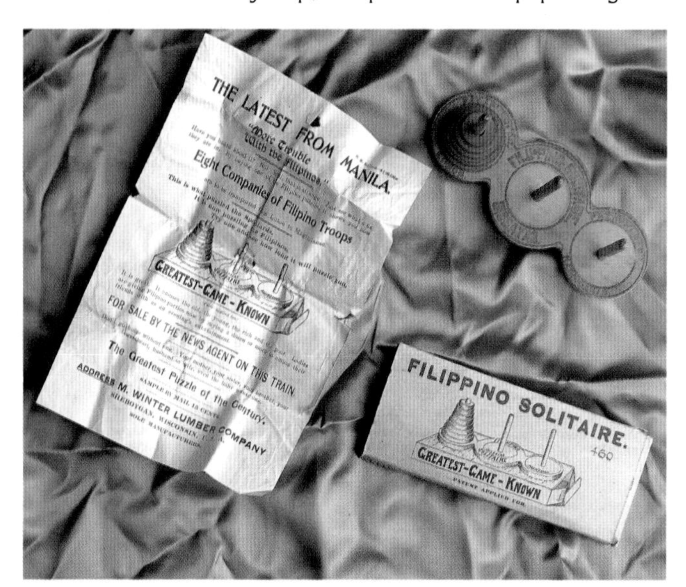

555

556

PAPER

Of all the many kinds of penny toys discussed in this book, the paper toy is the most difficult to pin down, since the different forms it came in are so vast and, frankly, many of them cannot really be defined as a toy.

For the sake of simplicity only paper items played with by children have been included. Thus the enormous subject of children's books, chromo-scraps, hats, masks and board games are strictly speaking not in the mainstream of our subject and have been thoroughly dealt with by other more learned authors in recent years, such as Iona Opie (29) and Blair Whitton (45). However, we must touch on some of these items briefly, since they were in their time considered as penny toys.

CUTOUTS

The earliest paper toys were the cutout card sheets which could be made up into toys. The greatest of these, by far, were the 'Imagerie d'Epinal' and Pantin by the printer Pellerin in France. From the beginning of the 1800s right through Victoria's reign and up to the First World War, every subject under the sun could be cut, folded and glued into accurate models and toys. The 'Planches d'Epinal' reflected the Industrial Revolution as it unfolded – balloons, sailing ships, trains, paddle steamers, horse carriages, dreadnoughts, the motor car and omnibus, and finally the submarine and the aeroplane, all came and went as paper cutouts, leading to the introduction into the English language of the saying "Penny plain, tuppence coloured".

There were, of course, many other printed sheet manufacturers throughout Europe. Surviving examples of cutout toys can be found from Denmark, Italy, Germany, Austria and in England (34), where Pollocks with their many different paper cutout theatres established a long tradition of paper toys, one that is happily still with us at Pollocks Toy Museum and shop in London.

Many of these cutout toys could be made to move with sand, a candle or later an elastic band. Mobile pictures were a speciality of Pellerin.

CHROMOLITHOGRAPIC SHEETS

Known as scraps or reliefs in England and America, chromos in France, glanz-bilder in Germany and many other names around Europe.The skills for engraving lithographic stones in Germany were the same skills which produced the flat tin soldier. Invented in 1837, the year of Victoria's Coronation, by Godefroy Engelmann, the chromolithographic process of printing in many colours, with a seperate stone being used for each colour, was the greatest step forward in printing since Caxton 400 years before.

The original chromo scraps were not cheap; 6d to 1/- per sheet in the 1850s was common and at such a price children were not the real buyers. Rather they were intended for use as a new form of colourful decoration for screens, boxes, valentines and, in Germany, on the special 'Oblaten' biscuits traditionally associated with Easter, christenings, weddings and Christmas.

From the 1880s, when etched steel plates replaced the heavy litho stones and mechanical steam presses took over from the hand-operated 'swinging weight' presses, the price dropped dramatically from 80 shillings per 100 to the same per 1,000. This is exactly 1d per sheet which is why they soon became known as 'Penny Reliefs'.(3)

Although nearly all the actual printing, embossing and piercing was carried out in Germany, principally in Berlin and Leipzig, the artwork and design was produced in England, France and America. Among prominent scrap publishers in London were Birn Bros, Davidsons and Charles Lee. But by far the largest was Raphael Tuck & Sons, an international printer and pioneer of many new innovations in the use of scraps, especially for children's toys.(45)

557 Paper construction toys by Raphael Tuck, 1890

It was Tuck who first made stand-up chromo figures from the American Civil War in the 1860s, then of the Sudan war heroes, Gordon, Wolsley and Stewart. In 1885, their series of Kings and Queens of England with their seals and coins – 37 in all – were an educational milestone. To celebrate Victoria's silver Jubilee in 1887, Birn Bros commissioned Harry Payne to paint a series of 12 stand-up reliefs of her reign and also 12 Victoria Cross heroes.(3)

Tuck's first real paper toys were produced in 1890 and represented a London omnibus and a furniture removals van, both horsedrawn. These large colourful reliefs quickly slotted together to make a fully three-dimensional toy – much like an 'Epinal' but without the need to cut them out. (**557**)

The Boer War generated a whole series of stand-up tableaux, sold as seperate sheets or as a set of six for 6d. They featured the armoured train, balloons, Boers ambushing, field ambulance and nurses, and NSW Lancers. After 1905, Tuck produced many series of fold-up nursery rhymes and fables. About 1910, small story books appeared with a concertina of scraps which could be cut free to stand up on cardboard bases. Besides fairy tales, there were farms, zoos, birds and toy soldiers. The set of 10 could be bought in a special gift box for 1/- or singly at 1d each. (**558**)

One sheet of scraps depicted the Edwardian seaside treats, most of which cost 1d in the early 1900s – donkey rides, ice cream, Punch and Judy, deckchairs and the delightful scene shown on page 172 of the 1d balloon seller.

PAPER DOLLS

In France, the paper Pantin was a familiar toy to children and adults alike. The Pantin was a dismembered figure printed on paper or card and coloured, originally by hand but later by blocking and finally by the lithographic colour process.

When the figure was cut out and the torso and limbs pinned together, it became an animated puppet or 'Jumping

558 Penny paper books

Jack' which could be made to move by pulling a string. An English printer is credited with the 'invention' of superimposing layers of interchangeable cut out clothes onto a paper figure in the 1790s. (45) The interest in cut out dolls and clothes soon spread to France and Germany. Pellerin was quick to exploit this new toy by issuing several sheets of 'Poupées à habiller' – female figures with dresses, cloaks, wigs, hats and accessories in the latest 'Empire' fashion. The company also printed Napoleonic grenadiers and the Imperial Guard with interchangeable uniforms.

The concept of the paper cut out doll crossed the Atlantic with the flood of immigrants during the 1840s and 1850s. The earliest known examples of American printed dolls were produced in 1857 by Clark, Austin and Smith in New York. By the late 1870s, several American companies including McLoughlin Bros and Milton Bradley were printing vast numbers of cut out doll sheets each year. These ranged from large dolls with elaborate costumes which were expensive down to the penny paper doll range.

The largest company, McLoughlin Bros in their 1882 catalogue list more than thirty sets of 'Penny Paper Dolls' which retailed at one cent each (actually 1/2 penny sterling). These penny dolls were uncut, folded sheets of stiff card measuring approximately 125 mm x 330 mm, both coloured and plain in an outer wrapper. Subjects included Dolly Varden and family, Tom Thumb, dressed animals, nursery rhyme characters and five girls called Amelia, Emily, Martha, Julia and Isabelle, each with three dresses. The 1882 catalogue also lists sets of soldiers for 'the amusement of boys to cut out'. From the 1890s onwards, some American magazines and regional newspapers started to include weekly sheets of cut out dolls which could be dressed in the latest fashions. Many of the doll designs were syndicated across the United States. The heyday of these give-away 'penny dolls' was between 1895 and 1920.

THE MULTUM IN PARVO CO.'S
Revised List of Games
WHOLESALE ONLY.

Chameleon, 1/-, a Game for the Chess Board.
Turnover, 1/-, the Reversible Counter Game for the Chess Board.
Shop, 1/- Musical Dominoes, 1/-
Birds, Beasts, and Fishes, 1/- Music, 1/-
Fairy Tales, 1/- The Stock Exchange, 1/-
Judge & Jury 1/- Newmarket, 1/-
The Dockyard, or Table Ship-building, 1/-; also at 6d.
Merry Families, 1/-; also at 6d.
Who Buys? (the Auction Game), 1/-; also at 6d.
Word Making & Working Taking, 1d. 2d. 3d. 4d. 6d. 1/- 1/6 2/- 2/6
The Poets' Conversation Cards, 6d. & 1/-
Money Matters, 6d. & 1/- Tennis, 1/- Nap, 1/-
Four Flags, 1/- Animal Quorum, 6d.
Simple Games for Simple Folk, 6d
Penny Games, 6 Sorts. Penny Packs of Playing Cards.
Twopenny Games, 6 Sorts.

FOR ILLUSTRATIONS SEE OVER.

NOTE TO THE TRADE.—We shall be pleased to lend the above Blocks for illustrating Catalogues, Lists, or Pamphlets, FREE OF CHARGE.

559 Multum in Parvo sales sheet

BOARD GAMES

Most of us are familiar with board games like Snakes and Ladders, Ludo, Halma, Chinese Chequers, Draughts, and many

560 Two penny games

561 A group of penny games

others. We played them in our childhood and like riding a bicycle, once learned you never forget. What we probably do not realise is not only how ancient most of these games are, but how adaptable the Victorians were in creating new board games based on these simple competitive principles as typified above all in the old French goose chase game 'Jeu de l'Oie'.

Ludo is a centuries-old game, originating with the Indian game, Parchees, while Halma came back from Turkey after the Crimean War. The Victorians and Edwardians were inveterate inventors of new board and table games. Literally hundreds came onto the market every year, often to succeed for a few years, but most to fail and, after losing their inventors money, they would sink into oblivion. A few went on to last forever such as PIT, Lexicon, L'Attaque and Happy Families which are still played today. (45)

The problem with board games is that they have lots of bits, so the printer is obliged to put them in a stout box, often with compartments. This made these games surprisingly expensive; most often cost more than a shilling, which was a lot of money in 1900.

The major printing companies which produced games were Chad Valley, John Jacques & Sons, and JW Spears in England and Parker Bros, Mcloughlin Bros and Milton Bradley in America; with Spears being also active in Nuremberg.

Nevertheless, there was a cheap end to the market, necessitated by the fact that the vast majority of the population wanted to play games but could not afford the high prices. On the one hand considerable effort was taken by these large printers to patent and copyright their games, while on the other equal amounts of effort was employed by others to pirate and plagiarize them. Accordingly certain games companies produced 6d and 1d ranges of games to capitalize on this popular demand.

One example is the 'Multum in Parvo Co' whose sales sheet is shown in plate **559**. While most of their games, invented

562

by Mrs Allison, were sold for one shilling, they also list "Penny Games 6 sorts, Twopenny Games 6 sorts and Penny Packs of Cards". Unfortunately, what these games were, we'll never know, as this kind of cheap ephemera, printed on low quality board paper, just gets lost or thrown away.

The very few survivors are, therefore, of considerable interest to historians. Plate **560** shows a couple – Black Peter comprised eight matching pairs of ugly people and one odd Peter card, the new Game of Nationalities (note the price of only 1/2d) comprised 6 sets of cards of different European nations with which to play Snap or Rummy.

Most stationers, village shops and market stalls would have a surprisingly wide choice of 'New Games' in the penny range, such as those shown in plate **561**. With these, the purchaser was apparently expected to provide the counters and dice for play. Since the box was the most expensive part of the game after the board, to dispense with it brought the price down dramatically. There was consequently a brisk turnover of these 'new games', which needed little invest-

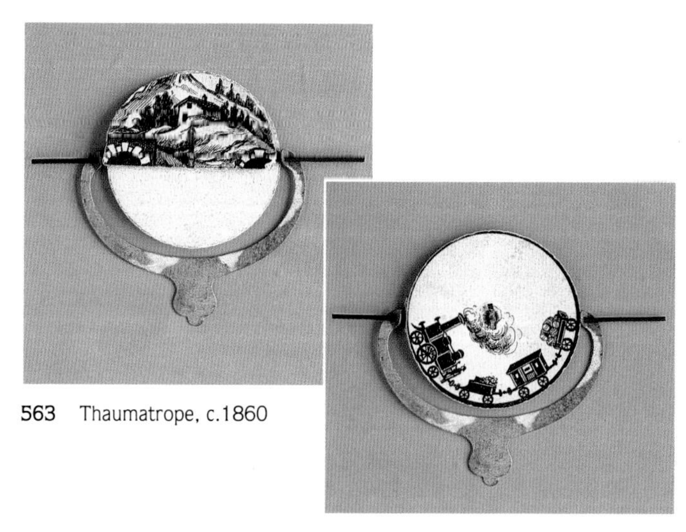
563 Thaumatrope, c.1860

ment and no patenting, as they were plagiarized and could be changed rapidly as events and fashion dictated.

There was, therefore, a glut of motor car, travel and race games from 1904 to 1910, which had replaced a spate of train and army games (the Soldier Boy game in plate **561** still shows red-jacketed infantry fighting the Boers). The craze from 1909, not surprisingly, was aeroplane games and impossible flights of fancy were flown around the world until 1913/14 generated hundreds of patriotic war games yet again.

The one shilling box of a dozen penny games in plate **562** is from the 1913 Gamages catalogue.(1) It must have been a bestseller, as a very similar box of 1d games was in the 1906 catalogue seven years earlier.(48)

Even politics generated board games. There is one of about 1913 which lampoons the Suffragette Movement. You lost turns by being chained to railings, going to prison and going on hunger strike. Whichever party paid the printer, Tory or Whig, they were undoubtedly male chauvinists!

PAPER PUZZLES, TEASERS AND MOVERS

Just as our grandfathers' families enjoyed parlour games, so they loved puzzles and brain teasers even more. This was the age of the conundrum, the riddle, the limerick, the crossword, the jigsaw, Sherlock Holmes, 'Tales of Mystery' and the unimaginable future of Jules Verne and H G Wells.

At the turn of the century, children and adults alike, were fascinated with puzzles, optical illusions, magic, practical jokes and tricks of every kind. A W Gamage at their Holborn Emporium had a whole department devoted to childish humour, practical jokes and the amateur magician – their 1906 catalogue has no less than 35 pages devoted to tricks.(48) It is little wonder then that the puzzle, trick, illusion, teaser and mobile were an enormous penny toy market whose demands were insatiable.

One of the earliest optical illusion toys was the Thaumatrope, invented in 1825. It was a popular penny toy right through to 1900. The example shown in plate **563** would

564 Mechanical penny bank

565 A selection of penny mechanical pictures

date from the 1860s, judging by the style of the locomotive. When spun, the locomotive appears to move into the tunnel which is on the other side of the disc. Most other optical inventions were much more expensive than a penny because they were dependent on rotating drums, mirrors or viewing lenses.

Another popular cheap toy was the 'Metamorphose' – strips of paper where the head, arms, body and legs could be changed to produce many comical characters. An example is shown at the left of plate **561**.

The King collection contains many paper penny toys. The selection shown in plate **565** are all pictures which have movement, usually by rocking the frame. Thus, Scotch Willie waddles across the stage, the horses jump on their springs and the musicians play when one pulls and pushes a tab.

Another interesting penny toy found in the King collection is the Kicking Mule moneybox shown in plate **564**. Surprisingly it combines in one toy all the materials that have been discussed in the previous chapters. It has a cast flat lead body, tinplate legs, a wooden base and a paper tube for the money. According to King's records this unusual toy, which embodies the same idea as the American cast iron Mechanical Banks, was bought on 7th December 1895.

A collection of small box puzzles shown in *The Golden Age of Toys* (34) and made between 1900 and 1915, illustrates what a wide range of penny puzzles and teasers were available. England, Germany and America all generated their own characteristic products. Some of the German made items came in several language versions, so international was the market.

Just as with board games, so puzzles could be political. The one shown in plate **566** shows a famous British Politician, Joseph Chamberlain, MP (father of Neville Chamberlain, the Prime Minister of Munich fame), who was well known for his monocle and orchid buttonhole. Chamberlain

566 Penny political puzzle

resigned his cabinet post in 1903 to campaign for Imperial Tariff Preferences for the British Empire. The two opposing characters in this puzzle are the USA, represented by Uncle Sam, the Trade Protectionist, and Bismark, the German Chancellor and Free Trader. The same argument is still with us today, except now Germany has been replaced by Japan as the Free Trade protagonist.

One thing is certain – the penny toy in all its different forms was no respecter of trade barriers. It was truly the universal expression of childhood.

3

IDENTIFICATION

THERE ARE four basic methods of identifying the maker of a penny toy: by trademark and inscription, through wholesalers' catalogues, through a study of component parts and, finally, by style alone.

Of the four methods, the last is the most uncertain and subjective, requiring a good knowledge and feel for penny toys. It is hoped that this book will have helped their identification become a little easier.

A Meier box lid showing the dog and cart and JPM trademarks

TRADEMARKS & INSCRIPTIONS

MOST PENNY toys have some form of printed or embossed trademark or inscription on them. This is the best and easiest guide to identification. The following is a guide to some of the marks that are commonly found on penny toys or the box lids that contained penny toy sets.

HENRI AVOIRON

The embossed initials HA usually found on the base of the penny toy were the trademark of Henri Avoiron. This company which was the successor to Petitnicolas, 53, Rue Rébeval, Paris was active from 1893 to 1922. In 1909, they advertised "Jouets roulants et routières tels que cheval, éléphant, lion, chameaux, polichinelle, locomotive, autobus, etc pour le 0 Fr 10." The toys are invariably spirit-painted and some incorporate lead castings (see 489).

JOSEPH BISCHOFF

The crossed swords and initials J B was the trademark of Joseph Bischoff of Nuremberg. It was first registered in 1899. Bischoff was a toy soldier maker who sold penny toy type vehicles in boxed sets along with lead soldiers. It is not known whether Bischoff made any of these penny toys or whether they were bought in from other manufacturers (possibly Hess).

JOHANN DISTLER

The trademark with the thistle and or the monogram JD was used prior to 1914 and again immediately post-1918. In the early 1920s, the initials JD were used on their own but in the late 1920s the trademark of the globe with the initials JDN was used.

Johann Distler commenced production of tin toys in Nuremberg about 1900. The pre-1914 production was dominated by penny toys but in the 1920s and 1930s the penny toy production was secondary to larger scale tin toys.

DRGM

Standing for Deutsches Reichs-Gebrauchs Muster, this mark signifies a second grade or utility patent expiring after three years, or more rarely six. These initials are occasionally seen on German penny toys.

DRP

Standing for Deutsches Reichs-Patent, this mark signifies a full German patent. If present in conjunction with a number this is a very useful guide to dating the toy, as patent numbers were issued in chronological order. It is rarely found on penny toys.

GEORG & JOHANN EINFALT

This Nuremberg maker, founded in 1922, did not trademark the simple penny toy beetles, butterflies, tortoises, etc, which were an important part of their production in the 1920s and 1930s. Many Einfalt penny toys found in the United States bear the UTCC logo.

IJF

An as yet unidentified trademark. This possibly French manufacturer made a range of lithographed animals on wheeled bases and an attractive race car (149).

JOSEPH FALK

Joseph Falk commenced business in 1897 in Nuremberg making mainly steam accessories and boats. However, Falk did make boxed sets of small toys for the bath which included fish, ducks, frogs and boats. These were usually made of zinc, hand-painted and were penny toy sized. They are very difficult to distinguish from the similar looking Uebelaker products. The Falk trademark of a tower with the initials JF within an oval may be on the box lid label.

GEORG FISCHER

F or GF was the trademark used by Fischer on pre-1914 penny toys. In the 1920s and 1930s, the monogram GF was used. Most later Fischer toys are marked but many pre-1914 examples are not and they can be difficult to identify.

Georg Fischer commenced production in 1903 in Nuremberg. Distribution seems to have been entirely through wholesalers. A wide range of fine quality, imaginative penny toys were made prior to 1914. Fischer was second only to Meier in the quality and range of penny toys made. It is possible that the trademark FZ could be an early Fischer mark.

GES. GESCH

Standing for Gesetzlich Geschutzt, this mark is frequently found on penny toys by Meier, Fischer and occasionally other German manufacturers. It signifies that all or some part of the toy is covered by a patent. Meier usually printed this inscription on an inconspicuous part of the penny toy.

HESS

The initials JLH, either individually or in a monogram, on a penny toy signify that the maker was Johann Leonard Hess. The company was founded in 1826 in Nuremberg by Matthias Hess and continued after his death in 1886 by his son. Penny toys were a relatively small part of the Hess factory production. The principal penny toys made were trains but road vehicles were supplied to other companies to use in sets.

ISSMAYER

Founded in Nuremberg in 1861 by Johann Andreas Issmayer, this company produced in the nineteenth century a large number of small, hand-painted, brass toys such as ducks, fish and boats. They were also magnetic and could float. These were never trademarked but originally came singly or in small boxed sets with the Issmayer trademark on the instruction

leaflet or box. These are one of the true precursors of the classic lithographed tin penny toys. With the increasing use of offset lithography from the late 1890s onwards, Issmayer began to produce small sized train sets and automobiles, some of which can be considered true penny toys. They were rarely if ever marked on the toy itself, but when sold as a boxed set the trademark sometimes appeared on the box lid. Issmayer was renowned for the quality and clarity of its lithography.

Issmayer appears not to have sold toys directly but worked through wholesalers or distributors. Bing, Carette and Schoenner catalogues of the early twentieth century all feature penny toy type trains made by Issmayer.

SAINT MIHIEL JEUNE

Founded in Paris in 1880 as Saint Mihiel, this company had evolved into Saint Mihiel Jeune by 1906 and by 1922 it was called Saint Mihiel Fils. Publicity pages for 1911 show a penny toy car, plane and train. The only confirmed Saint Mihiel Jeune penny toy illustrated (**237**) is a simple, spirit-painted train set in a box with a marked label. The toy itself is of a type much earlier than its early twentieth century manufacturing date and is unmarked.

MADE IN JAPAN

Many different Japanese companies made tin penny toys in the 1920s and 1930s. Many of these companies have not been identified, although others such as CK (Kuramochi) are well known for their larger toys. The marks illustrated are from some of the toys depicted throughout the book. Most bear their maker's mark and also the inscription 'Made in Japan'. When

unmarked, Japanese tin penny toys are usually recognizable by their bright colours and their non-Germanic feel. Many are copies of German penny toys.

Japan also produced vast quantities of wood, paper and plaster penny toys, which are usually impossible to attribute to any specific manufacturer.

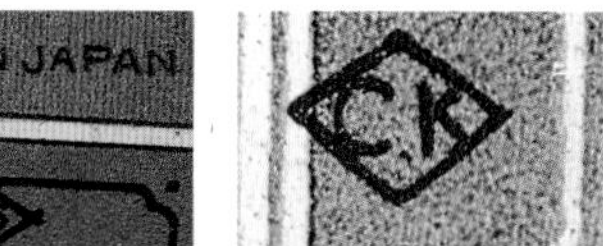

GEORG KELLERMANN

The CKO monogram often with a reference number was found on many, but not all, Kellermann toys. The company was founded in Nuremberg in 1910 and produced penny toys both with and without clockwork. Kellermann was a significant penny toy producer in the 1920s and 1930s and was particularly well known for its range of motorcycles.

HUBERT KIENBERGER & CO.

KI-CO was the trademark of the company in which Hubert Kienberger and Georg Levy were partners. Founded in 1910, this company made a small range of penny toys. The trademark was not often used and the penny toys can be difficult to identify.

GEORG LEVY

Georg Levy was a partner in Kienberger and Co. until 1916. After the end of the First World War, he founded his own company manufacturing penny toys and other cheap mechanical toys. The penny toys were rarely marked and can be difficult to identify. A series of row boats with one, two or four scullers were the best known Levy penny toys.

The larger mechanical toys were frequently marked with the trademark of a double pool player and the word GELY. The company was sold in 1934 when Georg Levy emigrated to England.

MEIER

Johann Phillip Meier founded the company that bore his name in 1879 in Nuremberg. In 1894, the dog cart trademark was registered. The earliest Meier toys were spirit-painted, frequently of embossed tin and never trademarked. Often the only guides to identification are the wheels and the quality of manufacture which was always high. In the 1890s, lithography was gradually introduced. At this period some toys were entirely spirit-painted, some had lithographed parts and others were all lithographed. By 1900, lithographed toys dominated production. Johann Meier died in 1911. From this date onwards, the quality of production started to decline until by the 1930s Meier was no longer a quality manufacturer.

Inflation was a significant cause of Meier's quality decline in that it was no longer possible to use the best quality tinplate and to replace worn lithographic plates when needed. Economies had to be made in order to still be able to sell toys for a devalued penny each. Johann Phillip Meier must have been such an innovative perfectionist to have produced the quality and range of penny toys available in the early 1900s, that it is hard to imagine that he would have permitted boring, poor quality toys to have ever left the factory that bore his name. It cannot be coincidental that quality appears to have started to decline from the date of his death onwards.

Meier was almost exclusively a penny toy manufacturer who sold to wholesalers, chocolate and sweet makers and other toy makers. Many lithographed Meier toys are trademarked with one or more of the illustrated marks. The dog cart mark was frequently embossed into the tinplate. When no trademark is present the best guides to idenfication are the wheels or the presence of GES. GESCH discreetly marked in the lithography. Fischer and other makers occasionally used this mark, but Meier was the most frequent user. The company ceased trading in 1934 or 1935.

HMN

An as yet unidentified penny toy manufacturer (probably Nuremberg based), whose penny toys feature on page 345 of the 1926 *Universal Toy Catalogue* under reference 2035/4. The only one trademarked is the early touring car illustrated in plate **134**.

PARKER BROS INC.

This American company based in Salem, Massachusetts and New York, was a significant importer of penny games and boxed sets that contained tin penny toys. These boxed sets (see plates **3** and **4**) contained penny toys made by Meier, Distler and Hess. These sets were printed and made in Nuremberg by JW Spear & Son and were directly marketed in Europe by them. When sold in the United States, these sets bear the Parker Brothers imprint and no mention of JW Spear or their German origin.

No tin penny toys are directly marked by Parker Brothers.

PAYA

Founded by Hermanos Paya in 1906 near Alicante, Spain, this company is still in production and has recently re-issued a few penny toy fire engines that are basically identical to their 1930s production.

Paya produced a wide range of penny toys in the 1920s and 1930s, many of which were very similar to German penny toys. It is possible that some of Meier's tooling was bought by Paya. The current re-issued fire engines have basically the same pressings as Meier's pre-1914 series (see 208, 210). Many Paya penny toys have no trademark but if marked will have either an HP monogram or the name Paya.

ROSSIGNOL

Founded in Paris by Charles Rossignol in 1868, this company made many penny toys in the early 1900s that are spirit-painted and may have the initials CR embossed into the tinplate. In the 1920s and 1930s, Rossignol made a series of lithographed penny toy vehicles.

J W SPEAR & SOHNE

JW Spear & Sohne was a Nuremberg company best known for its games which were distributed worldwide. Their range included penny games and boxed sets, including tin penny toys as described under Parker Brothers.

UEBELACKER

Leonard Uebelacker founded his company in 1871 in Nuremberg. Although not strictly a penny toy manufacturer, some of their small boats and bath toys are close to being penny toys. The small boats were never trademarked, were always hand-painted and are very difficult to distinguish from those made by Falk. The toys were usually sold in boxes and positive identification is usually only possible when they are found with a trademarked box lid.

UTCC

The Universal Theatres Concession Company of Chicago commissioned many different penny toys from Germany to be made incorporating their UTCC mark.

Many penny toys made by Einfalt and Levy in particular from the 1920s and 1930s are found with either the UTCC initials or a fuller description as shown. These toys were sold with candy or as a boxed set or given to children as a favour in the foyer of theatres in the United States. The UTCC orders must have been very large, as a high percentage of Einfalt and Levy penny toys found in the United States bear the UTCC mark.

WHOLESALERS' CATALOGUES

MOST WHOLESALERS' catalogues feature a few pages of penny toys. The original manufacturer is rarely given, but frequently the manufacturer's trademark is visible thus providing positive identification. In *The Universal Toy Catalogue* of 1924/26, each manufacturer has been given a code thus:

Levy	2007
Distler	2009
Hess	2011
Einfalt	2014
Kellerman	2016
Meier	2018
HMN	2035
Fischer	2061
Ki-co	112

Generally each maker's toys occupy a page or group of pages, making identification easy. However, certain penny toys by different makers can be very similar. The engravings are normally very accurate indeed and careful study must be made.

In other wholesalers' catalogues, the above coding is not used and careful detective work may be required. In any wholesaler's catalogue it is normal to place similar items from any given manufacturer together and if on a page of penny toys several can be identified as being from one manufacturer, the chances are good that the remainder will be from the same manufacturer. Individual penny toy makers generally did not issue their own catalogues. Those makers whose main business was larger toys, however, frequently included some penny toys in their catalogues. In these latter cases identification is straightforward.

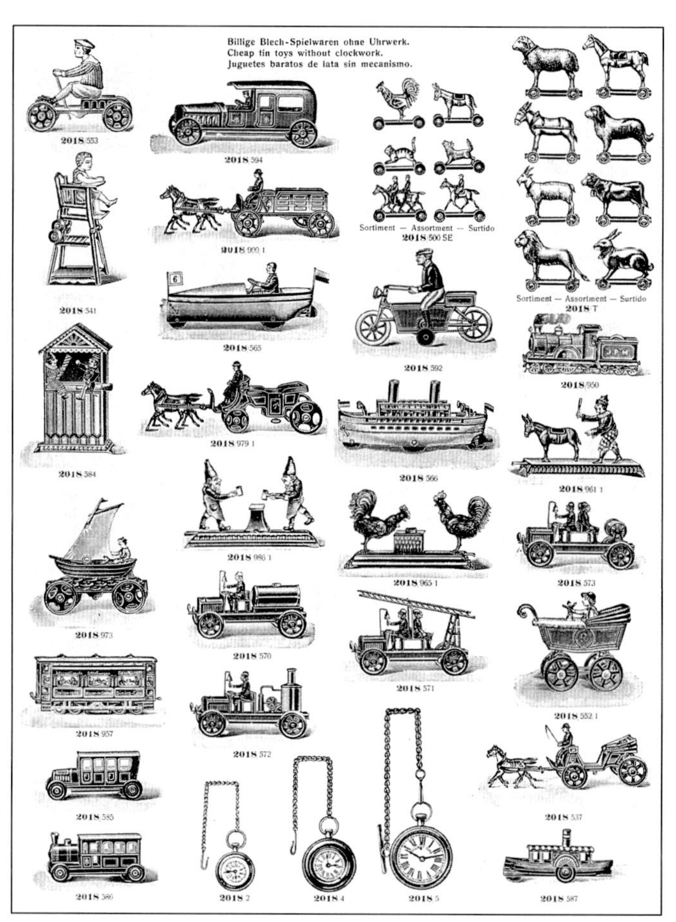

Meier penny toys from the 1924 *Universal Toy Catalogue*

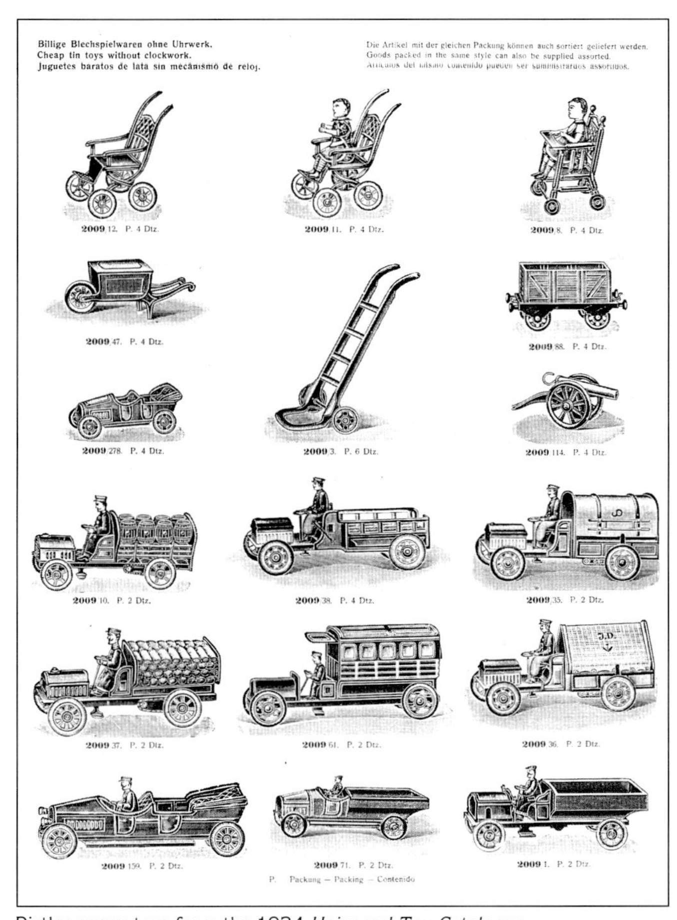

Billige Blechspielwaren ohne Uhrwerk.
Cheap tin toys without clockwork.
Juguetes baratos de lata sin mecánismó de reloj.

Die Artikel mit der gleichen Packung können auch sortiert geliefert werden.
Goods packed in the same style can also be supplied assorted.
Articulos del mismo contenido pueden ser suministrados assortidos.

2009/12. P. 4 Dtz.
2009/11. P. 4 Dtz.
2009/8. P. 4 Dtz.
2009/47. P. 4 Dtz.
2009/88. P. 4 Dtz.
2009/278. P. 4 Dtz.
2009/3. P. 6 Dtz.
2009/114. P. 4 Dtz.
2009/10. P. 2 Dtz.
2009/38. P. 4 Dtz.
2009/35. P. 2 Dtz.
2009/37. P. 2 Dtz.
2009/61. P. 2 Dtz.
2009/36. P. 2 Dtz.
2009/159. P. 2 Dtz.
2009/71. P. 2 Dtz.
2009/1. P. 2 Dtz.

P. Packung — Packing — Contenido

Distler penny toys from the 1924 *Universal Toy Catalogue*

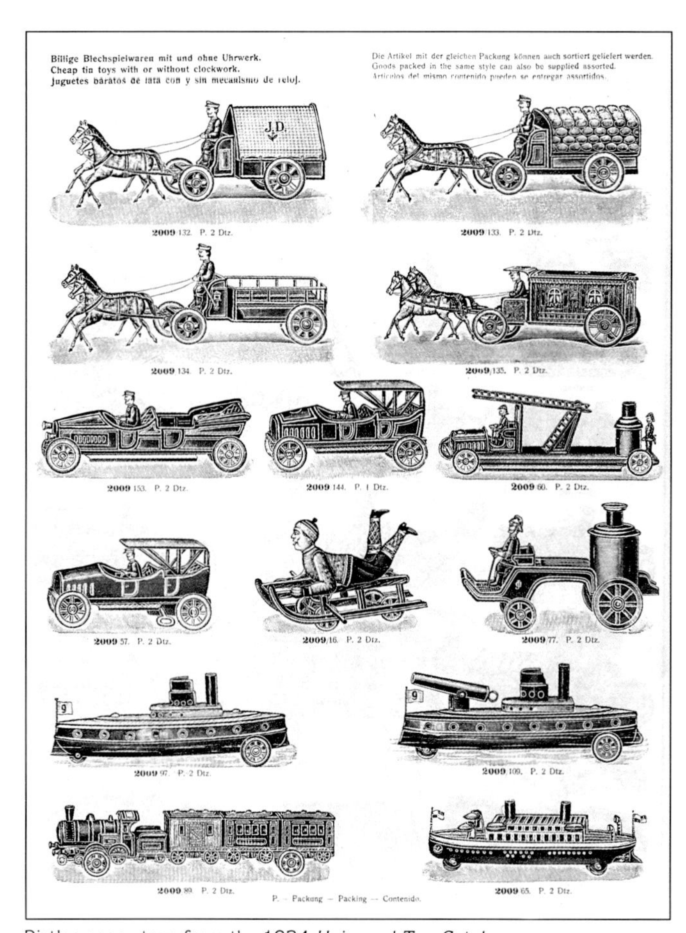

Billige Blechspielwaren mit und ohne Uhrwerk.
Cheap tin toys with or without clockwork.
Juguetes baratos de lata con y sin mecanismo de reloj.

Die Artikel mit der gleichen Packung können auch sortiert geliefert werden.
Goods packed in the same style can also be supplied assorted.
Articulos del mismo contenido pueden se entregar assortidos.

2009/132. P. 2 Dtz.
2009/133. P. 2 Dtz.
2009/134. P. 2 Dtz.
2009/135. P. 2 Dtz.
2009/153. P. 2 Dtz.
2009/144. P. 1 Dtz.
2009/60. P. 2 Dtz.
2009/57. P. 2 Dtz.
2009/16. P. 2 Dtz.
2009/77. P. 2 Dtz.
2009/97. P. 2 Dtz.
2009/109. P. 2 Dtz.
2009/89. P. 2 Dtz.
2009/65. P. 2 Dtz.

P. — Packung — Packing — Contenido.

Distler penny toys from the 1924 *Universal Toy Catalogue*

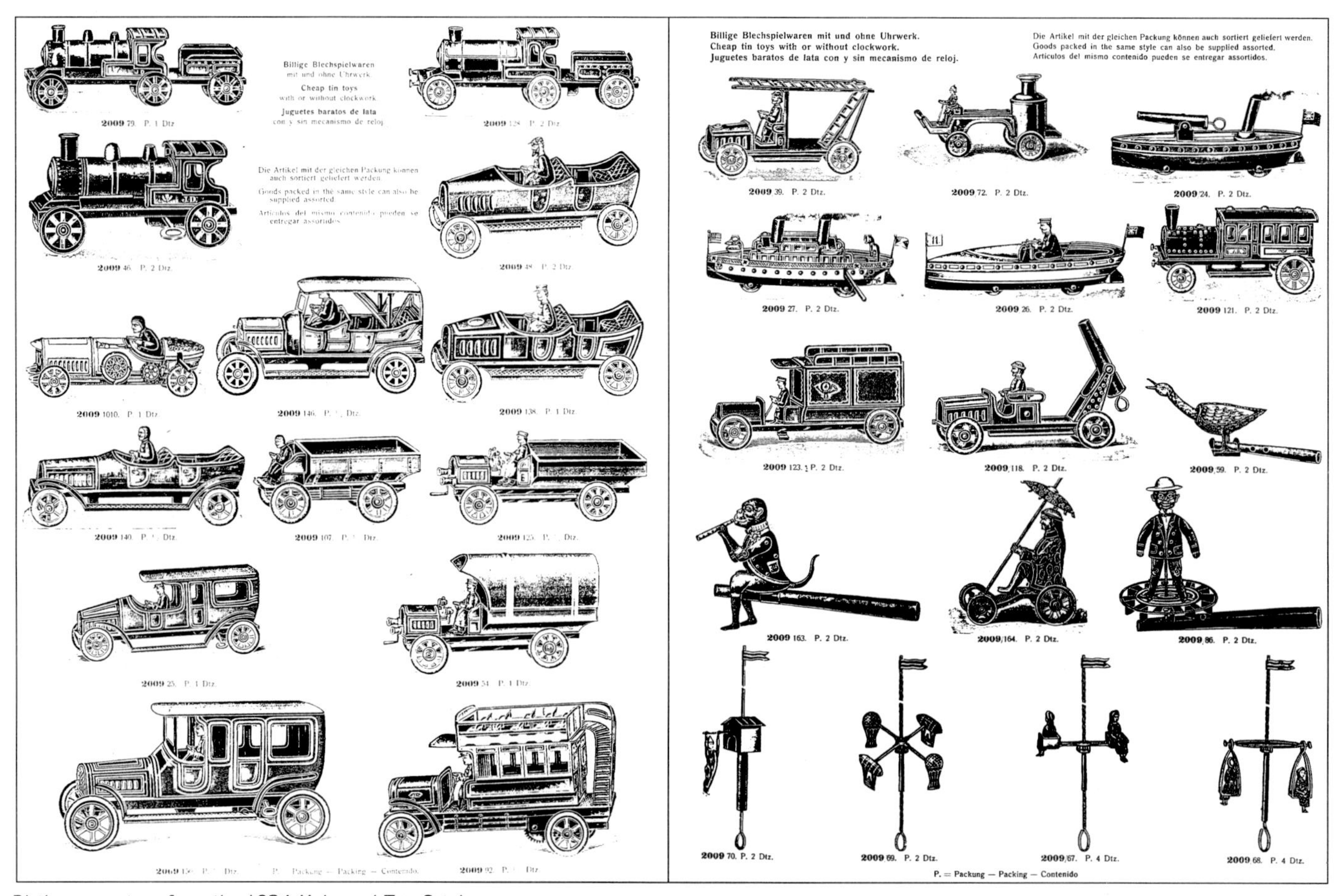

Distler penny toys from the 1924 *Universal Toy Catalogue*

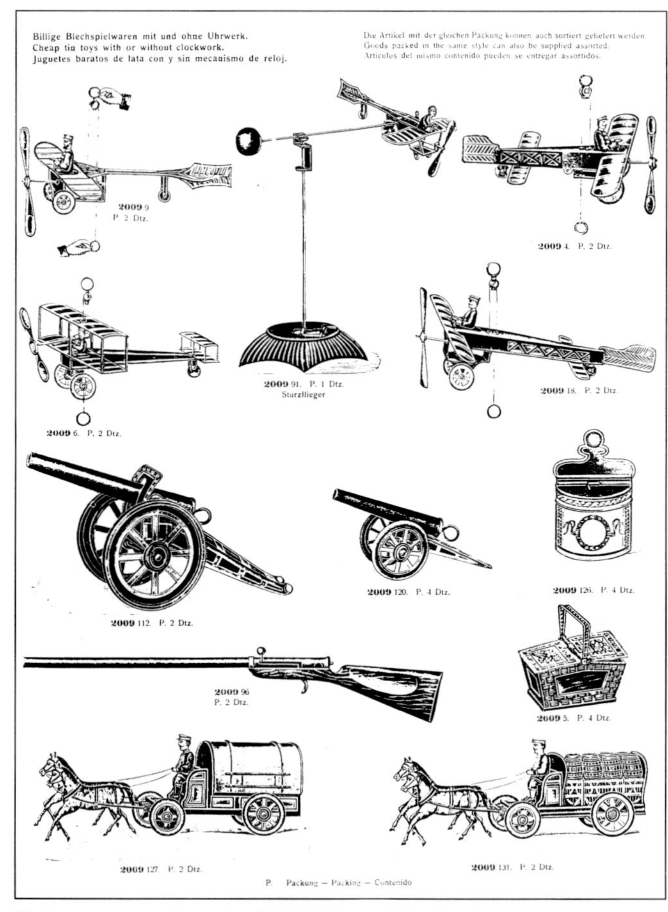

Distler penny toys from the 1924 *Universal Toy Catalogue*

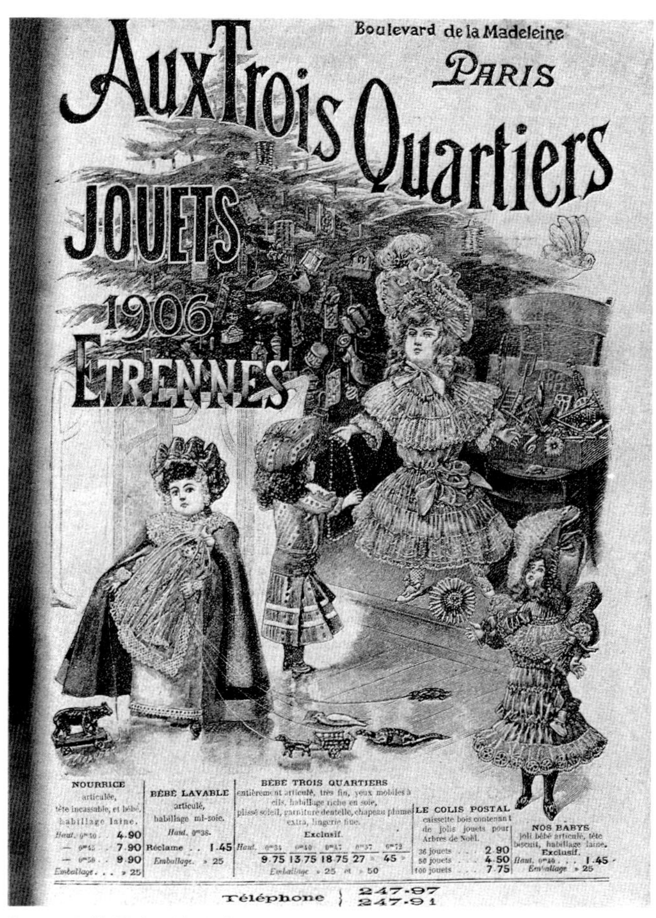

Cover of 1906 Aux Trois Quartiers department store catalogue showing an open box of mixed penny toys

COMPONENT PARTS

METHODS ONE and two can provide a confirmed identification quickly. Method three is only used if methods one and two have failed, as it can provide strong evidence but an element of hypothesis must still remain in the attribution. All penny toy manufacturers used certain parts for more than one penny toy. In the case of the major manufacturers, Meier, Fischer and Distler, the same parts, such as horses or a baseplate, might be used on a great many different toys. Penny toys were designed to be quick and easy to assemble. Consequently they are quick and easy to disassemble. In making an attribution from a study of component parts, the researcher must be satisfied that parts have not been changed. It is easy to change drivers, wheels, horses, etc on penny toys. It is not infrequent to find an attractive penny toy missing, say two wheels. It is easiest to remove four wheels from a damaged penny toy and fit them. This is not unreasonable but if the new wheels are from a different manufacturer, this could lead to attribution problems in the future.

Thus one must be cautious in definitive attributions based on removable parts. In the pre-1914 era, the major manufacturers had distinctive wheel patterns. By the 1920s the wheels all look very similar and positive identification from a study of the wheels is less certain.

Very distinctive early (circa pre-1905) wheel used by Meier. Available in several different sizes all of which featured the rather unstable hub in which the hub is tabbed onto the wheel from the inside out. This feature was exclusive to Meier.

Two styles of wheel with stable lead hubs to attach the wheels to the axle. Both styles were used by Meier from about 1905 to about 1914. The use of a lead hub was typically Meier and is found in very few non-Meier penny toys. Meier used these wheels in different colours. (above and right)

Typical lead centred wheel used by Meier on pre-1914 road vehicles. In later years, Meier used tin hubs outside the wheel much in the style of Distler and Fischer.

Fischer used this distinctively shaped wheel for many years in several different sizes. The tin hub has four tabs that turn inwards to hold the wheel. Distler used a similarly shaped wheel for a short period in the 1920s.

Typical Distler six-spoke wheel from the pre-1914 era. As with Fischer hubs, the outside hubs are held on the wheel with four tabs. This became virtually standard practice for all manufacturers in the 1920s. Most French made penny toys had spirit-painted cast wheels with six spokes.

Two examples of simple disc wheel used by Meier

BIBLIOGRAPHY

The numbers refer to text references in Part 2 Other Materials

Published books

1 Adburgham, Alison, *Gamages Christmas Bazaar*, David & Charles, 1974

2 D'Allemagne, Henry, *Histoire des Jouets*, Libraire Hachette et Cie, 1903

3 Allen, Alistair & Hoverstadt, Joan, *The History of Printed Scraps*, New Cavendish Books, 1983

4 Baecker, Carlernst & Haas, Dieter, *Die Anderen Nurnberger Band I – VII*, Hobby Haas, 1973-88

5 Bellu, René, *Les Autobus Parisiens*, Jean Pierre Delville, 1979

6 Brett, Bernard, *History of World Sea Power*, The Military Press, Hamlyn Publishing Ltd, 1985

7 Britains Ltd, *Wm Britain's catalogue 1910*, Facsimile, 1972

8 Cadbury, Betty, *Playthings Past*, Praegar Publishing Inc, 1972

9 Corredor-Matheas, J, *La Joguina A Catalunya*, Edicions 62 SA, 1981

10 Craig, Gordon, *Book of Penny Toys*, 1899

11 Dearmer, Mabel, *The Book of Penny Toys*, Macmillan, 1899

12 Erfut Musser, Cynthia, *Precious Paper Dolls*, Hobby House Press Inc, 1985

13 Fritzsh, K E & Bachmann, M, *An Illustrated History of Toys*, Abbey Library, 1966

14 Garratt, John G, *The World Encyclopaedia of Wooden Soldiers*, Muller, 1981

15 Gottschalk, Lilian, *American Motortoys*, New Cavendish Books, 1986

16 Griffith, David, *Decorated Printed Tins*, Studio Vista, 1979

17 Hollingswood, Brian & Cooke, Arthur, *The Great Book of Trains*, Colour Library Books, 1987

18 Howard, Marian B, *Those Fascinating Paper Dolls*, Dover Publications, 1981

19 Jeanmaire, Claude, *Bing, Grandad's Model Railway*, Verlag Eisenbahn, 1972

20 Johnson, Peter, *Toy Armies*, B T Batsford Ltd, 1981

21 Kurtz, H Z & Ehrlich, B R, *The Art of the Toy Soldier*, New Cavendish Books, 1987

22 Lamming, Clive, *Les Jouets Anciens*, Atlas, 1982

23 Lamming, Clive, *JEP Le Jouet de Paris 1902–1968*, Adrian Maeght, 1988

24 Lienser, Thelma, *Economic Statistics (UK, USA, France, Germany) 1900–1980*, Bank of England, 1983

25 Longest, David, *Character Toys & Collectables*, Schoeder Publishing Ltd, 1987

26 Mace, L H & Co, *Illustrated Catalogue 1907*, Washington Dolls House & Toy Museum, 1977

27 McKenzie, Ian, *Collecting Old Toy Soldiers*, B T Batsford Ltd, 1975

28 Milet, Jacques & Forbes, Robert, *Toy Boats*, Charles Scribner's Sons, 1979

29 Opie, Iona & Robert, *The Treasures of Childhood*, Pavilion Books Ltd, 1989

30 Parry Crooke, Charlotte, *Toys Dolls Games – Paris 1903–1914*, Denys Ingram, 1981

31 Parry Crooke, Charlotte, *Mr Gamage's Great Toys Bazaar 1902–1906*, Denys Ingram, 1982

32 Prendergast, Curtis, *The First Aviators*, Time Life Books, 1981

33 Pressland, David, *The Art of the Tin Toy*, New Cavendish Books, 1976

34 Remise, Jac & Fondin, Jean, *The Golden Age of Toys*, Edita Lausanne, 1967

35 Remise, Jac, *L'Argus des Jouets Anciens 1850–1918*, Balland, 1978

36 Remise, Jac & Remise, Frederic, *Encyclopedie des Jouets – Les Bateaux*, Pygmalion, 1981

37 Remise, Jac & Remise, *Frederic, Encyclopedie des Jouets – Attelages, automobiles et cycles*, Edita Vilo, 1984

38 Schroeder, J J, *The Wonderful World of Toys, Games and Dolls 1888–1930*, D B I Books Inc, 1971

39 Stannett, Vivian, *Cellulose Nitrate Plastics*, British catalogue of Plastics, 1979

40 *Universal Toy Catalogue 1924–26 Facsimile*, New Cavendish Books, 1985

41 Welland, James & Force, Edward, *Tootsie Toys*, Motor Books International, 1980

42 Weltens, Arno, *Mechanical Tin Toys in Colour*, Blandford Press, 1977

43 White, Gwen, *Toys Dolls, Automata, Marks & Labels*, B T Batsford Ltd, 1975

44 White, Gwen, *Antique Toys and their Background*, B T Batsford Ltd, 1971

45 Whitton, Blair, *Paper Toys of the World*, Hobby House Press Inc, 1986

46 Wragge, D, *Flight with Power – First Ten Years*, Barrie & Jenkins Ltd, 1978

Magazines, periodicals, catalogues and unpublished material

47 *Antique Toy World*, monthly

48 Gamage A W Ltd, 1906 catalogue

49 *Illustrated London News*, Christmas 1957

50 International Antique Toy & Doll Convention catalogue, 1982

51 *Childhood* exhibition catalogue, Sotheby's, 1988

52 Stollwerck's Preis Liste and catalogue, 1901

INDEX

Type of toys

INDEX

Poem and illustration from *The Book of Shops* by E V Lucas and F D Bedford

KERBSTONE MERCHANTS

Some people make collections
  Of fossils, eggs and ferns
Of coins, and stamps, and butterflies
  And other things by turns.

But Uncle's more original
  Than anyone you'll meet,
For he collects the penny toys
  They sell you in the street.

Wherever crowds are thickest
  These merchants stand all day,
With every kind of 'novelty'
  Spread out upon a tray.

And Uncle takes his business bag
  And buys from every one,
Though he once bought a running mouse
  And couldn't make it run.

E V Lucas, c.1905